John Williams Walker

A STUDY IN THE POLITICAL, SOCIAL AND CULTURAL LIFE OF THE OLD SOUTHWEST

HUGH C. BAILEY

John Williams Walker

A STUDY
IN THE POLITICAL, SOCIAL AND CULTURAL LIFE
OF THE OLD SOUTHWEST

UNIVERSITY OF ALABAMA PRESS

University, Alabama

To Mother and Father

Acknowledgments

I WISH TO ACKNOWLEDGE MY INDEBTEDNESS TO SOME OF the numerous individuals who aided in the preparation of this study. I am indebted most to the late Dr. Frank L. Owsley, Sr., who directed the original study of Walker's life which was submitted as a doctoral dissertation at the University of Alabama. As counselor and friend, Dr. Owsley challenged me to pursue the study and guided and criticized the work over a period of months. I trust that some of his scholarship is reflected in these pages. Dr. Charles G. Summersell and Dr. James B. Sellers, erudite writers in the field of Southern and Alabama history, also read the work, and it contains a number of corrections made at their suggestion.

Librarians too numerous to mention aided me during the decade of research for this book. I am particularly grateful to Mrs. Vivian Lawson of the Reference Department of the University of Alabama Library, Miss Josephine Cleveland, Miss Della Dryer, and Miss Jessie Ham of the Birmingham Public Library for their unending patience in obtaining materials. The study could not have been written without access to the rich resources of the Alabama Department of Archives and History, Montgomery, where invaluable assistance was given by Miss Frances M. Hails.

At the Duke University Library, Miss Mattie Russell of the Manuscript Division was most helpful in locating Walker correspondence, while at the Howard College Library, Mr. F. Wilbur Helmbold and Miss Helen Stamps assisted me.

I am grateful to all those who have given generously of their time and labor to make possible the writing of a manuscript. I am also grateful to the staff of the University of Alabama Press and to Mrs. Eunice H. Payne, its Editor, for efficiency and uniform kindness.

HUGH C. BAILEY

Birmingham, Alabama

Contents

ONE

Background

IN AUGUST 1773, THE REVEREND JEREMIAH WALKER, Baptist preacher extraordinary, pastor of the Nottoway Church of Amelia County, Virginia, and intermittently minister of half a dozen other infant churches, was in jail. According to the Chesterfield County Court he was guilty of "sundry misdemeanors" the most heinous of which was preaching to the people without benefit of ordination in the Church of England. It would be early September before, pleading his own cause, he would argue so cogently as to gain his freedom. Jeremiah's ability to convince the Chesterfield authorities would have caused little surprise among his congregations. At 26, he had already commanded more respect and love from the simple folk of the Virginia backcountry than most men twice his age.

Jeremiah had been born, the son of immigrants, in North Carolina in 1747. Just seven years earlier his father, William Walker, had emigrated to Maryland from Ireland, where the Scotch-Irish Walkers had held Anglican parishes since the early seventeenth century. First of the Walkers to cross the Irish Sea had been George Walker, who became Rector of the Anglican Parish of Badoney in County Tyrone. His success here led to appointments as Rector of Kilmore and Chancellor of Armagh.

The Chancellor's son, George Walker, II, his education at Glasgow University embellished by an innate opportunism, rose to great heights in the Church. Marriage into the influential Maxwell family of Scotland advanced him, and a bold stand in behalf of William and Mary at the time of the Glorious Revolution played its part. George held rectorships in the Diocese of Armagh and in County Tyrone in 1688. From these he raised and equipped fifteen companies of sixty men each to meet the invasion of the deposed James II. After the withdrawal of James' defeated army, the Rector journeyed to London to present an address of loyalty to the new sovereigns on behalf of the citizens of Londonderry. As a personal reward, the grateful William and Mary bestowed on him a purse of £5,000 and the Bishopric of Derry, one of the most valuable of the Irish sees.[1]

It was the Bishop's great grandson, William Walker, who found life in Ireland so unrewarding that in 1740 he made the voyage to Maryland. Then, at some date before 1743 (we do not know when) William Walker moved into that section of North Carolina west of the Chowan River known as Bertie District. Here, on March 30, 1743, he presented to the governor's council his headright claim, for himself, his wife Ursula, and two other dependents. He was granted 200 acres of land,[2] and on it he settled.

The area was often called "the south side of Roanoke." In the 1730's and 40's Virginia migrants poured into the region, seeking better lands than the exhausted ones of eastern Virginia. Many were educated and cultured and promptly sought to reproduce the society they had known in the Old Dominion. Governor Josiah Martin, writing in 1772, felt the settlers here were so different from other

North Carolinians that one would be led to think them
people of another region.³ On the other hand, some of the
migrants were former bondsmen who quickly claimed up
to 640 acres of land for their families under the North
Carolina headright system and frequently found ways to
obtain much more.⁴

To the William Walkers a third child, Jeremiah, was
born in Bertie District in 1747,⁵ and, like the other Walker
children, he received a sound basic education. There is no
evidence that he went to college, but he could express
himself with clarity and even with eloquence.

Most of Jeremiah's adult life was spent as a Baptist
minister, a turn of events which may seem surprising in
view of his distinguished Anglican ancestors and the fact
that the Church of England was the established faith in
Virginia and North Carolina. But Jeremiah lived as a child
and young man in that peculiar spiritual vacuum which
had developed in the Virginia backcountry and in all of
North Carolina. The English Church, and indeed most of
western Christianity, reached a low mark in the eighteenth
century. Plagued with deistic thought and not yet re-
juvenated by the Evangelical and Tractarian movements,
America's "Mother Church" was in no position to conquer
a wilderness. The lack of an American bishop seriously
limited its ministrations, since confirmation and ordination
could be obtained only by a transatlantic voyage. The
number of clergymen was appallingly small, and the few
that did exist, for the most part English-born and English-
educated, were scarcely equipped to cope with the idiom of
the upcountry masses. Their task was the more difficult
because after several generations of neglect, any knowledge
the people had of the Church's teachings and customs had

disappeared. Often regions developed without ever seeing a copy of the King James Version of the Bible, much less *The Book of Common Prayer.*

It is true that parishes were laid out on the map, and there were some who worked with great fervor in enormous Church districts. Yet too often only the wealthy, educated, and socially pretentious few responded, and the Church which prided itself in being "the holy Catholic faith for English speaking peoples" often was anything but universal above Tidewater.

Into this religious vacuum in the eighteenth century South came the Baptists, followed in a few years by the Methodists. Before the end of the century, they had reached a towering numerical superiority everywhere in the interior—a superiority which they retain today.[6]

From 1695 on, North Carolina had seen a spectacular growth in the number of those holding Baptist beliefs—i.e., separation of church and state, baptism of believers only, limitation of church membership to those having a "regenerating" conversion experience. The fourth Baptist Church in the state, Reedy Creek Church, was established in 1750 in Bertie District, where the Walker family had settled. In the next few years Daniel Marshall and Shubael Stearns, both of whom had been converted in New England under the influence of George Whitfield, began to preach in upcountry Virginia and North Carolina. Under their influence, the young Jeremiah Walker was converted at a revival held at Sandy Creek Church in Guilford County, and at 21, he was conducting religious services as an ordained minister for the Separatist Baptist groups in North Carolina and in Virginia.

He went into Amelia County, Virginia, for the first time in 1768, and although the services he conducted were illegal, almost immediately, the denomination began to grow at a greatly accelerated rate.

Baptists had first appeared in Virginia in 1714, and in Amelia County in 1765. As the church grew—perhaps because it grew—its conflict with the law began. Supposedly the Act of Toleration granted the right to worship to all Protestant Trinitarians, but Virginia law required licenses for any meeting of such a religious group. In the late 1760's and 70's licenses were repeatedly denied Baptists, and on November 28, 1768, the Amelia County Court refused a petition to license the Walker gathering.[7] Shortly thereafter actual persecution of Baptists began. But the Baptist movement continued to grow, becoming so strong in the backcountry that it could no longer be ignored. Now it began to attract not just the very poor, the illiterate and uncouth, but people of a higher class, and the lowcountry was aghast. A 1768 letter to "The Irregular Baptists" in the *Virginia Gazette* reveals something of the loathing with which followers of this group were viewed. It noted that "the modern Baptists" had for some time "been the instigation of considerable disturbances, whose insignificance perhaps, rendered them beneath the notice of the learned world." It seemed to be necessary to offer some evidence "in opposition to their insipid Divines" to retard their "divisive progress" which was dangerous among those "not well acquainted with Divine truths." The writer was most critical of Baptist rejection of all human learning, which many held was not only unnecessary "but highly destructive in a gospel Minister." He felt that if Baptists needed only inspiration to proclaim the truths of Christianity they were "very self-confident," and if they did use human learning they were "liars." "If the blind lead the blind, both shall fall into the ditch," the writer concluded.[8]

Though the *Gazette's* description fits many Virginia
Baptists of the time, particularly those of the more numerous, Calvinist-minded Separatists, it does not fit Jeremiah Walker. Walker, although ostensibly a Separatist was
really Antinomian in his view and "renounced the tones,
actions and violence characteristic of Separatist Baptist
preachers and discouraged the outcries, ecstasies, and ep-
ilepsies so much thought of by them."

Yet his moderation was no handicap to his career. Under
his preaching 66 persons were induced to form Nottoway
Church near the banks of Nottoway Creek, and Walker
moved from North Carolina to accept the pastorate in
1769. For the next fifteen years he retained this position
and, despite the severe trials he encountered, enjoyed
marked success.[9]

The Nottoway Church prospered from its inception. It
followed the Baptist custom of encouraging members who
lived at some distance to establish independent churches,
and Walker often served as pastor of these new congregations. Thus, he served the Sailor Creek Church when
Nottoway members formed churches in northeastern
Prince Edward County. He was the first minister of
Meherrin Church, organized in 1771 from Nottoway members in Lunenburg, Mecklenburg, and Charlotte Counties
as the first Baptist Church in the area. As a result of
revival tours he made, other new churches sprang up. In
1773 he organized the first Baptist Church in Dinwiddie
County from among believers to whom he had preached for
a number of years on itinerant preaching missions. Once
more he agreed to serve for a time as minister of that
congregation. Again, he was able to influence other preachers to help found new churches. His persuasion was
instrumental in leading William Mullen to establish the

first Baptist Church in King and Queen County in 1769.[10]
And all the time his own Church thrived. By 1773 Nottoway Church had 200 members, despite its losses to newer
congregations and Walker's frequent absences to minister
to them.[11]

It was natural that Walker should assume a leading role
in the formation of the Virginia Association of Separatist
Baptist Churches. Before 1771 all Virginia congregations
had been affiliated with the Sandy Creek Association in
North Carolina, but in that year twelve churches in eleven
Virginia counties chartered the association. Walker served
as a messenger to the meeting and preached to crowds
estimated at from 4,000 to 5,000 persons.[12]

Just two years earlier Walker had been sued in two
actions in the Lunenburg County Court by the father of
Henry and Lester Bryan for baptizing his two minor sons.
The action was eventually dropped, although there is some
doubt as to whether the court costs were paid by Walker or
by a friend of the Bryan family.[13] But now new conflicts
with the civil authorities began to plague the minister.
Although the Lunenburg County Court granted the request of a Baptist petition for a place of worship in 1770,
it was not until February 25, 1772, that the House of Burgesses agreed to a petition of Lunenburg County praying
that the benefits of the Toleration Act be extended to
Baptists. After deliberating for thirteen days, the Committee for Religion of the House resolved that Baptists
should "be treated with the same kind Indulgence in
religious Matters as *Quakers, Presbyterians,* and other
Protestant Dissenters."[14]

Nonetheless, regular persecution of Baptists which had
been initiated in several counties about 1768 continued
and was vigorously pursued even by such distinguished

men as Edmund Pendleton and Archibald Cary. And, in 1773, Walker was arrested in Chesterfield County and tried before the County Court "for sundry misdemeanors [upon his] acknowledging that he had convened the people in this county and preached to them not being a minister of the Church of England." The justices ruled that such conduct was "a Breach of the Peace and of Good Behavior" and ordered him to "the Gaol" of the county until he should "enter into Recognizance himself in penalty of £50 with To [Two] Sureties in penalty of £25 each for his Behavior for the space of one year nex [sic] ensuing."

In the Chesterfield jail Walker joined another Baptist minister, John Weatherford. The bitterness of the civil authorities over their clerical activities extended beyond the letter of the law and contributed to their misery. On September 3, when the court learned the two ministers had been allowed the liberty of the prison bounds, they were ordered to be placed in close confinement—a piece of brutality remedied only by the intercession of Patrick Henry. Not long after, "Walker pleaded his cause under the Act of Toleration so conclusively that he was discharged," but Weatherford was kept for five long months and then freed only because Patrick Henry secretly paid his jail fees. Although a Churchman, Henry was a sincere friend of dissenters, and did much to secure them the protection of the laws. Somewhat later he defended three Baptist ministers imprisoned in Spottsylvania County. Henry's attitude toward dissenters perhaps explains some of his hold on the backcountry masses.[15] Jeremiah Walker owed much of the success of his later career to the progressive ideas of this liberal Virginia patriot.

TWO

Revolution and Removal

DAVID BENEDICT, A LEADING BAPTIST HISTORIAN, BELIEVED the persecution of Jeremiah Walker was the heart of a plan to destroy the most troublesome dissenters in Virginia. If the civil authorities could silence "so distinguished a man among the despised Baptists," lesser voices would shortly be extinguished also. If this were the plan, the strategy failed.[1]

Obviously, Walker was a symbol of the best that the Baptist denomination had produced. Both Semple and Benedict describe his engaging manners. "Gentle, affable, polite; cheerful yet grave, familiar yet dignified," he could "ply his competitor with strong arguments" while appearing to be neither urgent nor positive in manner.[2] His "patience, humility, and uniform prudence and piety, acquired for him the esteem of all whose prejudice would allow them to think favorably of a Baptist."[3] He had "arrived to a degree of distinction far above any of his associates. In whatever direction he might travel, he was hailed by many as father in the gospel." He was "caressed by his friends" and "admired by all, even his enemies" and was invited into the polite society of Virginia's "great" families. Among the Baptists, of course, he was "all powerful," especially in their associational meetings.[4]

At the joint meetings of the district associations in 1774, Walker's qualities were put to the test. After prolonged debate, it was agreed to establish the office of "Apostle," whose duty would be to oversee the spiritual work of the associations and go among the people strengthening and sustaining their faith. Walker's championship of an office so similar to the episcopate in functions, if not in theory, is overt evidence of his conservative theology. The office was abandoned after one year, but it is rather remarkable that a predominantly Calvinist group would establish it at all.

The question of predestination almost split the meeting. Walker, Samuel Harris, and John Walker vigorously set forth the Arminian contention that Christ died for all men who would accept his grace. They were opposed by John Williams, William Murphy, and a number of others. The dispute became so intense that the Arminian group withdrew, and communication was continued in writing. Eventually, however, a compromise which settled no basic theological questions restored fellowship. Fellowship, the Calvinists stated, "seems nearly as dear to us as our lives," but its restoration might never have occurred had it not been for the esteem in which Walker was held.[5]

In the quest for religious freedom, however, there was no division among Virginia Baptists. The first organized action for separation of church and state in Virginia was taken at the associational meetings in 1775. Walker and three others were appointed to present an address to the General Assembly requesting that it grant all ministers liberty to preach to the troops at any convenient time they chose "without molestation or abuse." On the motion of Patrick Henry, the Assembly approved the request, and Walker, among others, spent several months preaching to the soldiers without great success.[6]

During the course of the Revolution, Virginia Baptists conducted a continuous campaign for religious freedom. When Patrick Henry was elected Governor in 1776, they were at last assured of a friendly climate for advancing the cause of religious and civil liberties, and they hastened to take advantage of it. Thus, in December, 1776, ministers and delegates from Dover and Goochland counties thanked the General Assembly for enacting a law to exempt dissenters from taxation to support the Established Church. When additional rights were not forthcoming, the General Association, in 1778, appointed Walker, Elijah Craig, and John Williams to present the grievances of Virginia Baptists to the Assembly. In 1780 the Assembly received another memorial in Walker's handwriting, signed by him and 75 members of Nottoway Church. This asked that the vestries of the parishes, a vital unit in local government, be elected by all voters, and that dissenting ministers be allowed to perform legal marriage ceremonies. The exclusive right of the Anglican clergy to solemnize marriages was a particularly sore point. As early as 1775 the association meeting in Cumberland had protested, declaring marriage was a civil contract, and it was no part of the ministry "to marry persons."

In December, 1780, the Virginia Assembly reluctantly authorized the judges of the state to license four ministers of each sect in a county to perform marriage ceremonies and marriages previously solemnized by dissenters were declared valid. The action preceded by just six years the complete separation of church and state in Virginia. Walker, who had drafted many of the petitions of protest and supported them before the Assembly "where he gained the applause of the candid members as a man of sense and address,"[7] was largely responsible for the complete capitulation. In addition, he had personally contributed to the great growth of the Baptist denomination by founding between twenty and thirty churches south of the James River, and his ministry had been extended to many more. Everywhere he preached, large crowds of admirers greeted him.[8]

Yet despite his achievements in Virginia, Jeremiah Walker made the decision shortly after the Revolution to move to Georgia. It is evident that he was not happy with the increasingly Calvinistic theology of Virginia Baptists, many of whom regarded him as something of a fallen angel.[9] Very probably, however, economic, not religious, reasons persuaded him to make the trek south. In 1783, when John Williams Walker was born, Jeremiah Walker's family included five sons and one daughter.[10] It was no small task to provide for so large a family in postwar Virginia.

Virginians emerged from the Revolutionary War poor in purse and restless in spirit. Imprudent cultivation had exhausted the land; a legacy of war debts, the newly imposed and devastating British trade restrictions, depression of currency, and inflation in prices, all combined to produce "the worst financial depression that ever came into Virginia life." The state's paper had been demonitized as legal tender in 1781-1782 in order to combat the flood of paper money, and continental currency was virtually worthless. Even the planters were in desperate poverty. Thousands moved to the new lands of Kentucky, North Carolina, and Georgia even before 1786-1787, when the depression was at its worst.[11]

During the war, Colonel George Mathews had gone to Wilkes County, Georgia, and bought a large area of land known as the "Goose Pond Tract." The soil appeared to be very fertile and similar to that of the Virginia Piedmont.[12] The Colony of Georgia had purchased this area from the Indians in 1773, and the constitution of the new state established a liberal "headright" system under which each family head could receive 200 acres of land with an additional fifty for every child and slave (up to ten Negroes).[13] When Mathews returned to Albemarle County, Virginia, his enthusiasm for the Georgia tract spurred Francis Meriwether, Benjamin Taliaferro, and several others to visit Wilkes County in 1784. They purchased lands on this initial trip, and within the year they and many others, including Jeremiah Walker, had settled in Georgia.

Almost all those Virginians who came to the Broad River area were small planters or very well-to-do yeomen. For the most part they brought a few slaves, some cattle, books, and household furniture. From the beginning they were self-conscious, feeling themselves to be much more refined than other upcountry Georgians. Their sense of superiority and the fact that they had known each other in Virginia contributed to a tight-knit society in the area. The Gilmers, Meriwethers, Taits, Bibbs, Taliaferros, McGehees, Crawfords and Walkers maintained a community life here which was to influence the entire development of the Old Southwest.[14]

The social cohesiveness of the Broad River area may have stemmed in part from a singular economic unity. The virgin lands located at the confluence of the Broad and Savannah Rivers were ideally suited to the cultivation of tobacco, and the emigré Virginians made tobacco the basic crop. The area's principal town, named Petersburg after the Virginia city, developed rapidly in response to the demands of tobacco culture. Since state law required the inspection and payment of fees on all tobacco before it could be shipped, warehouses had to be erected and shops established. Before the end of the century, Petersburg had more than forty stores and warehouses operating near the rivers. Most of the region's tobacco was sold here to merchants who "from their full stores, supplied every need of the producers." Some authorities believe Petersburg's trade in the first decade of the nineteenth century was greater than that of Augusta, and certainly its citizens claimed that "goods of superior quality were sold at cheaper rates in greater quantities" than elsewhere in Georgia.

Most of the tobacco was floated down the Savannah River to Augusta and Savannah in long boats, pointed at the ends and round bottomed. Many of the purchases of the people were poled up the river, and many passengers who might shop in the city or travel north or abroad were carried.[15]

Wealthy Petersburg merchants built lovely homes in town and engaged in planting on the side, and, typically, many planters built their houses in town. The residential area was behind and well above the business section. Town lots were nearly three-quarters of an acre in size and were laid off at right angles to each other. A resident wrote in 1800, "It is a handsome, well-built Town, and presents to the view of the astonished traveller, a Town which has risen out of the Woods in a few years as if by enchantment." At the turn of the century it had, in addition to its stores and warehouses, a distributing post office, a market place, a town hall and 700 to 800 residents, "and was considered second in importance only to Augusta."[16] "For twenty years or more . . . [it] was noted for the intelligence and wealth of its inhabitants."[17]

Cotton killed Petersburg. By 1810 it had only 332 people, and in a few years it was extinct. The newer lands of the Southwest attracted a large part of the population. Those who remained in the region found it more convenient to ship their cotton direct to Augusta and Savannah from landings on the bluffs of their own lands. But Jeremiah Walker lived in tobacco's heyday in the Broad River region.

Beyond any doubt, Walker was a highly successful planter. According to the Tax Digest of 1785, he had already acquired 1,364 acres of land in Wilkes County and 2,733 acres in Washington.[18] In 1791 he purchased 190 acres on the north side of the road which ran from Petersburg to Tugaloo, and, apparently, all of Collins Island (approximately 356 acres of land) in the Savannah River.[19]

At the same time he continued his activities on behalf of the Baptists. The sixth Baptist Church in Georgia was Fishing Creek Church, established soon after the Revolution five miles north of Washington in Wilkes County. Jeremiah Walker affiliated with Fishing Creek Church and was in 1786 one of the founders of the Georgia Baptist Association. The same year, he was chosen clerk of the association and wrote its circular letter. In classical style he "bid welcome to Boanergers' [sic] thunder—Barnabas' consolation—Paul's argumentation—Appollos's eloquence—and Cephas' zeal." He rejoiced that "at length the two sticks are made one, by abolishing the nominal distinctions, *regular* and *separate,* which have long unhappily divided the Baptist Churches." Henceforth, he hoped Georgia Baptists would "Behold how good, as well as pleasant a thing it is for brethren to dwell together in unity."[20]

This hope was vain. Walker continued with the Georgia

Association for two years, but the prevailing Calvinism was at length more than he could bear. He persuaded the Reverend David Tinsley of Virginia and the Reverend Nathaniel Hall, pastor of two churches in South Carolina, to join with him in forming a General Baptist, or Arminian, Association. In all, six or seven churches defected from the Georgia Association to become affiliated with the new organization, but upon Walker's death it soon disbanded.

Religious disputes do not appear to have hurt Walker's prestige in the community. He was one of Wilkes County's two representatives to the Georgia Constitutional Convention of 1788 and was selected a justice of the peace in the same year.[21] At the time of his death in 1792, he was financially well-off.

All of Walker's possessions were left to his family. To Milly, his wife, went several slaves, his personal property, and one-third of the plantation. Polly Coleman, his daughter, received one slave whose progeny was to be divided upon Polly's death among her three daughters. His sons received more ample bequests. Henry Graves was given 400 acres of land, a town lot in Petersburg, and a slave. Memorable got 300 acres of land, some slaves, and some furniture. Jeremiah, named for his father, was the recipient of 150 acres of land on the south side of the Savannah River, part of Collins Island, and several slaves. James Sanders was given the rest of the island, 100 acres joining Jeremiah's land on the mainland, and a few slaves. A trust was set up for John Williams, who when he came of age was to have 250 acres of river land and several slaves. Elizabeth Marshall, the last of the Walker children, had received her portion of the estate before her father's death.

Upon each of the children, this scholarly father bestowed a share of his books.[22]

Most important, perhaps, Jeremiah Walker's children received from him, in addition to moderate fortunes, an initial training which influenced their entire lives. When their mother died a short while later, even the younger children, like John Williams, were able to cope to some extent with a vigorous, demanding society.

THREE

Youth

YOUNG JOHN WILLIAMS WALKER WAS ORPHANED AT THE age of nine and for the next decade was cared for by his four brothers. He was closer to Memorable, who served as his guardian, than to anyone else, and their love for each other seems to have been genuine and deep. From his brothers Walker learned much about agriculture, and, since Memorable and James Sanders were also Petersburg merchants, he became conversant with business practices while still in his teens. Although busy working in his brothers' store and, by the age of sixteen acting as collector of the debts of his friend Larkin Newby, Walker never allowed his studies to lapse. Late in 1803 he was to enroll in the Academy of Moses Waddell, a school which required good preparation. Meantime he studied, worked in the store, acted as Memorable's deputy in maintaining a post route through a portion of South Carolina, and served as Newby's agent after Newby moved to Fayetteville, North Carolina. Over and over again, perhaps because of the economic depression attendant with the Napoleonic Wars, he was forced to relay excuses instead of cash, but his persistence did bring Newby some returns.[1]

His family's respected position and his own decidedly social disposition qualified Walker for membership in the

"Junior Set" of Petersburg when he was seventeen, and before he was twenty he had risen to the senior group.[2] Though moral, he was not puritanical, enjoying an evening out with the boys where the "laughing tale and merry song" joined with the "quaffing [of] a bowl of delicious eggnog, or in an innocent game [of] whist" to bring joy to all.[3] He called on the most prominent young ladies of Petersburg and attended their parties, although initially he was always awkward and bashful. But he loved to dance, and once the ice was broken and the music began, "he shuffled a reel or hopped a Congo" with the best of them. He considered this his one advantage with girls.[4]

While possessing a warm and outgoing personality, Walker was keenly intelligent and liked to entertain himself by studying attitudes and customs around him. Something as important as the relationship between the sexes could never have escaped his careful consideration. When a friend expressed surprise that man should be taken in by woman, Walker informed him that this was only natural; somewhere, sometime it had been ordained that women should gain the affections of men and make themselves the object of their earthly adoration. "Else why were they formed more beautiful? Why are their natural dispositions formed to partake more abundantly of the milk of human kindness?"[5]

Through his early youth, Walker was continually under the influence of the "universal passion," never failing to "derive a pure, uncontaminated pleasure in contemplating the features" of his "heart's idol."[6] In his early formal education he attended a co-educational school, a most unusual arrangement for his time and locale, and he "had the advantage of prying into [the] native disposition of every female there." Here he became something of a connoisseur, if we are to believe his letters. Upon reflection, one girl who had long bewitched him lost her hold upon him when he perceived that she lacked "that inexpressible softness so lovely in a woman." He was attracted to another—so he came to realize—simply because she was not "ruffled by every blast of the pedagogical passion." In the summer of 1803 he turned his romantic interest away from yet another young lady when he realized that her mother's principal interest was her marriage to a rich man.[7]

During the Christmas season of 1803 when he was on one of his frequent trips into South Carolina, Walker was charmed by a Miss Betsy Nichols, whom he met at two balls on consecutive evenings in Cambridge. On one occasion he wondered if she were not the finest girl in the world. Back home in the new year, he was in greater and greater demand with the ladies. Untold empires beckoned when he found that he could extract "the honey from their very lips [with] their free consent." Obviously something of a student of female psychology, he wrote that he "found it no hard matter to persuade them they were handsome, for they thought so before; and you have nothing to do but flatter and deify a woman's beauty, and she will think you the finest fellow in the universe."

In retrospect, Walker decided that often he was nearer to being conquered than to conquering. On one occasion the young lady led him to kiss her, and the kissing was continued—and continued. "In short sir," he wrote, "I managed matters so devilishly well that I can say with Caesar, veni, vidi, vici." But as he made no exertion to gain this victory, neither did he "make any use of it," but, like an inexperienced general drew off his forces, and "suffered the enemy to recover from this dreadful shock."[8]

Earlier in this same year, Walker had become attracted, far more seriously, to the twelve-year-old daughter of a prominent Petersburg merchant. It seemed to him that the snow which blanketed Petersburg must have made this child jealous, since only it could equal the clearness and beauty of her "fair skin and lily white hands." The girl, who would one day be his wife, was Matilda Pope, the daughter of Colonel LeRoy Pope, one of the wealthiest men of the Petersburg area and a partner in the Walker brothers' business. In 1802 Colonel Pope had been appointed by the state one of the five commissioners who were to govern Petersburg. The Pope family was so eminent in the Broad River region, in fact, that it was known as "the Royal family."

Within the year Matilda was sent to Bethlehem College in Pennsylvania to complete her education.[9] Because of the prestige her family enjoyed and her extreme youth, Walker was hesitant of paying court to her directly. It was not difficult for him to find ways to be with her when she was in Petersburg, for her family entertained lavishly. The more he saw of her the more he loved her. In his opinion, she was not "the most exact, regular and beautiful figure in the world; not possessed of the most sparkling eye, ruby lips, or cherry cheeks"; neither was she what most people would call a beauty, but she did possess "a tender, engaging and lovely disposition," and a mind as yet "uncontaminated by the vain addresses and fawning attendance of worthy fops."[10]

He felt he could not marry for six years, since he wished to complete his education and establish himself first. But at the same time Matilda's absence gave him the most exquisite pain. He feared life in a Northern college would change her disposition, or "put high-flying notions into her head" which would modify her attitude toward former friends.[11] He worried, moreover, about the outcome of a long-standing, unsettled dispute between Colonel Pope and his father's estate, fearing that this would lead to a difference between them. Matty's father was a shrewd businessman and there were many who felt he took advantage of others in business relations. Walker knew if he were ever Pope's victim he would be forced to oppose him. "I like the man," he wrote, "I like his wife, I like his children, I *love one* of them, but I am determined never to crouch to him nor abandon my lawful right for the uncertainty of obtaining at a distant period, an amiable woman."[12] Fortunately a crisis on this issue never arose.

Despite the counsel of older, married friends that the love of youth is myth, Walker held that his feeling for Matty was true love since it was founded not on outward appearance but on temper, manners, and talents, "directed not to the gratification of sensual pleasure," but "elevated with the hope of [being] at some day master of so great a treasure."

The number of marriages taking place in Petersburg tortured him. "Egad! both men and women seem to be inspired with a determination to people the desert, to fulfill the purpose of their creation, and not die like 'pompion with the seed in their bellies!' " he wrote. "We shall soon have it in our power, if we go on at this rate, to send out a colony to Louisiana, without diminishing our present stock."[13] Though he railed about others, he in truth wished that he and Matty could join the parade.

But Walker's secret hope for an early marriage was shattered by tragedy. Two of his brothers, Jeremiah and Memorable, died in the same year. Family records give no indication of the cause of Jeremiah's death, but Memorable died of tuberculosis. Memorable had served as something of a substitute parent for Walker and "united, in a particular manner the character of a steady, warm and disinterested friend; a wise, virtuous, and incorruptible Guardian;—a bold resolute and determined protector." At the age of 29, he became violently ill. It may have been at this time that Walker contracted the disease, which haunted him the rest of his life, for he abandoned his other activities to stay at his brother's bedside, to offer what meager physical aid he could, and to give Memorable "opportunities of talking in an unrestrained manner." Memorable continued to suffer hemorrhages and paroxysms of coughing until his death April 27, 1803.[14]

Walker could find no words to express his grief. His love for Memorable was so great that he had refused even to contemplate the possibility of his death. Memorable had always been willing to impart his extensive knowledge, to relieve the distresses of the widowed, and to ameliorate the misery of the poor and the orphaned, and in matters of importance and delicacy, it seemed, the community of Petersburg had invariably turned to him. Walker believed if Memorable had lived, "the discriminating genius inherited from his father" would have made him "a great man."[15]

Mourning for Memorable, Walker tried without success to find solace in religion. Even though he was the son of a Baptist minister, he had adopted many of the concepts of the eighteenth century enlightenment which were current among the more intellectual in early nineteenth century America. Although Jeremiah Walker, Sr., had been a leading Baptist minister, his liberality had driven him to form a separate organization of churches. A tradition of dissent had become a Walker heritage.

The Methodist and Baptist faiths, predominant in the Petersburg area in 1803, were continually adding to their numbers through intensely emotional revivals. Highly conscious of the transitory nature of life immediately following his brothers' death, Walker could not accept the theology and practices found congenial by many of his neighbors. Yet he attended a number of revival services, since they were major local events. He commented with some sarcasm on one such meeting in which Sam Watkins and a Major and Mrs. Oliver joined the Methodist congregation. Then he added, "W. Watkins Carpenter [was] very loud" in his conversion. "Pate was on trial but failed by the way, being entirely too fond of whiskey."[16]

The itinerant Methodist preacher Lorenzo Dow, who roamed the countryside from New England to Louisiana preached in Petersburg in the fall of 1803. It was a part of his showmanship to announce that one year from a specific day he would preach under a certain tree in an area. He went from Petersburg to the Natchez area where he held the first revival southwest of Tennessee. In the Mississippi Territory he initiated his services in the usual way, by mounting the platform and crying out at the top of his voice that "he had heard the latest authentic news from hell and was going to publish it." After such an opening, his fiery sermons were apt to gain many converts.[17]

Walker had a measure of respect for Dow. He thought him "most contemptible" in appearance, "impeded in his utterance and of the most inharmonious voice," and felt that the oddity of Dow's manner was the substance of his fame, yet he conceded that Dow was "one of the soundest and most cogent reasoners" he had ever heard. He concluded that if a man had some ability "a departure from the beaten track of any profession (save perhaps Physic) would be attended with considerable profit."[18]

Three years after Dow appeared in Petersburg, Francis Asbury visited the town. Here he was startled and displeased to find that the Methodists had "instead of building a small convenient house" for use as a church, "bought an old house and fitted up a room for everybody." After calling on Charles Tait, a life-long friend of Walker, Asbury wrote in his diary that in visiting Judge Tait he presented himself as a Christian minister, not as a gentleman. He would visit the President of the United States in no other character, he noted. Perhaps their determination to show contempt for those who lived in some style does much to explain why Walker had a low opinion of the Methodist and Baptist movements.[19]

Nonetheless, the young Walker sought for greater insight in the field of religion. There is no record of his baptism, or his membership in any church, yet years later he was to write that he was a Baptist "by inheritance," and therefore his children could not be christened.[20]

At the time of Memorable's death, Walker found consolation in the thought that "the designs of the Almighty are unsearchable by man's comprehension." As the Reverend Moses Waddel read the words of Job at the funeral, Walker felt they proclaimed truth. "Man dieth, and wasteth away; yea, man giveth up the ghost, and where is he? As the waters fall from the sea, and as the flood decayeth and dryeth up, so man lieth down, and riseth not: till the heavens be no more, they shall not awake, nor be raised out of their sleep."

Fortunately Waddel for the most part "steered clear of the rocks of prejudice and intolerance and the quicksands of bigotry and superstition." At the end of his funeral sermon, he expressed the opinion that salvation comes only through "the merits of Jesus Christ," and Walker took exception to this, observing that "if that were . . . the case ⅘ of the world will inevitably be damned." Such a judgment would even have consigned Memorable, who was a deist, to hell, and Walker knew some better fate awaited his brother. "They say the hour of death is honest," he wrote. Feeling that no person could have met excruciating pain with greater fortitude than had Memorable, he was confirmed in the belief that "any man who conducts himself uprightly and by the dictates of his reason and his conscience will be happy hereafter."[21]

Though he openly avowed himself no deist and contended his views were not yet crystallized, he was reputed to be a deist among the Petersburg people. One evening when he rose to ask a question in church he was rewarded with a sermon blasting deists. Such experiences taught him never to dispute with those "incapable of permitting others to think and act differently from themselves." One must never oppose "the stubborn will of the ignorant, bigoted multitude" in order to acquire popular favor, he wrote.[22]

Both Memorable and James Sanders were deists and another brother, Henry Graves, believed "only parts." Thus, Walker was cast with them. His Uncle Dick alone did not consider him a deist, did not classify him "as a dangerous enemy to the Christian religion." Perhaps correctly, he thought him to be a Universalist.

Certainly the young man read widely in religious literature as well as in other fields. He found *Watson's Apology*, a reply to Paine's *Age of Reason*, a fine work and its author "a *gentleman* altho a *Bishop* and a follower of Christ." Volney's *Ruins* left the impression on him that "the

professors of every kind of religion [should realize] the
necessity of a *free, undisturbed toleration."* The ingen-
iously deistical *Philosophical Dictionary* was a delight
also.[23]

The more he read the more tolerant he became. He
advised a friend, in something of the credo of his life, "Be a
good man—Be religious if you choose, but do not be a
fanatical bigot."[24] In his personal life he was often flippant
and gay, his letters were sometimes risqué, but his morals
were impeccable. He challenged the views of some of his
friends who were "educated in the school of intemperance
and incontinency." He doubted that any sincere love
would ever lead a man to ruin "the peace" of a woman for
"the deceitful pleasure of a moment."[25]

When he was sixteen Walker refused to convey the
compliments of a friend to a school acquaintance who had
become a perennial card player, a deadbeat who was
completely dependent on the charity of his family. The
young moralist was thankful that he had been saved from
this fate by a modification of a course he had previously
pursued.[26] At twenty, his well-developed sense of ethics
caused him to cancel a profitable trade in cotton because
some objection was raised that he might be breaking a
contract. Perfectly sure that he was committing no offense,
he yet wished to avoid having "any stigma" affixed to his
name "by an uncandid world." He chose to avoid this risk
even though it meant a personal loss.[27]

But Walker's highly developed conscience did not rebel
against dueling. Duels were common in the Petersburg
area, and he was always interested in their provocation and
could be counted on to report their course in great detail.
When a Mr. McGrath defeated Litts Wilson in a wrestling
match in the late spring of 1799, the outcome brought a

challenge. Armed with pistols, the two men met across the Savannah River from Petersburg, but the affair came to an amicable end when a pardon was asked, and the duelists parted friends. Walker was delighted with the situation, feeling that conflict often preceded warm friendship. Had he and Newby not quarreled so often he was confident their friendship would never have been so warm and secure.[28] A year later two congressmen, James A. Bayard and C. C. Champlin, met, with only slight injuries. This duel had been provoked by a comment Champlin made on the floor of Congress in "the course of the debate respecting Negroes." About the same time, Major William Kersey of the Third United States Regiment was less fortunate; he was killed in a duel with a Lieutenant Marks of the same regiment. Concerning this affair, Walker had no word of reproach.

In other areas his righteous indignation knew no bounds. A Petersburg widow, a Mrs. Clark, was raped in 1800, and her assailant apprehended. After a trial he was sentenced to only one month's imprisonment, to pay a fine of fifty dollars, and to be pilloried. Walker felt that this was the least "reward the Villain Merited." Writing to Newby he asked that all such villainies be reported to him as it did his soul good to contemplate the execution of justice.[29]

Politics was another subject which fascinated Walker and Petersburg. The people of the Broad River area were "generally, republicans" and in particular was this true of Walker's social and economic equals. Walker was an apostle of Thomas Jefferson, but his detestation of the Federalists was not extended to his hero, George Washington, nor to his close friend, Federalist Larkin Newby.

Jefferson's acquisiton of Louisiana caused a Federalist uproar, but Republicans were jubilant. "This successful

termination of our embassy exceeded even the most sanguine expectation of Republicans" and should be a "powerful recommendation for Mr. Jefferson" to his fellow
citizens, Walker wrote. He had hoped a bipartisan approval
would hail the achievement. Federalists had contended in
Congress that the United States must acquire New Orleans
and control of the Mississippi, some even advocating war to
obtain them. They had accused the Republicans of "cow-
ardice and a want of determination to defend the honor
and liberties of our country." Now, Walker found, "when
we have obtained by amicable negotiations, what they
wished to gain by war, it is discovered that it will be
prejudicial to the interest of the United States to have so
vast a tract of additional territory."[30]

Newby argued that American diplomacy had failed since
it had not obtained precisely what it sought: the free
navigation of the Mississippi, the occupation of New
Orleans, and the annexation of the Floridas. Walker and
most of Petersburg disagreed. They were delighted with
the acquisition of all of Louisiana. Walker observed that
unless the United States held extensive bodies of land
along the Mississippi its navigation could be easily impeded
or absolutely stopped by any enemy who stationed some
ships at its mouth. Since the Floridas were Spanish, Petersburg Republicans reasoned they could not be purchased
from France, but "if the Spanish will dispose of them we
have every reason to expect they will soon be under our
jurisdiction."

Dr. William Wyatt Bibb, a neighbor and close friend of
Walker, was elected to Congress in 1803, at the age of 22.
Walker believed he would "perhaps do as much honor to
the country as any member" which the district had sent
"for many years" to Washington.[31] He was less pleased to

learn that Major Purviance had been elected from the Northern District, for a man named Hays had been his choice, "not only because he is a man of superior abilities, but because he is a Republican." He was glad, however, that Purviance defeated McFarland, whom he considered irresponsible in his personal life and lacking in talents, although a Republican. McFarland "embraces the right side of the Theatre of Public discussion," the future statesman wrote, "yet I should not hesitate a moment to vote in favor of" Purviance, because "a man dishonest in his private dealings can never be a real disinterested patriot."[32]

The same type of reasoning led Walker to condemn Burr and support the President in the Burr controversy. Before the former Vice-President's expedition had melted into obscurity, Walker was sure that it would not succeed. The activity of Edward Tiffin, Governor of Ohio, in seizing Burr's boats, and the work of the army which led to this seizure would cause the expedition "to end in smoke."[33] Jefferson's message to Congress explaining Burr's "treason" was a "most interesting document, full, clear and explicit." After Burr's capture Walker demonstrated a rare insight for the times by thoroughly distrusting General James Wilkinson, who he feared would allow Burr to escape.[34]

Walker's respect for Jefferson, however, did not blind him to the virtues of John Randolph, whom he greatly admired. When he heard a rumor that the great Virginian had been killed in a duel, he refused to believe it. "I know few men I should more regret" to see killed, he wrote. If this report were true, then a man of "talents and largeness and independence and patriotism and honor" had been removed from public life. When his Uncle Toby pro-

claimed, "He is not dead—'He shall not die *thus,* by
God,'" Walker chimed in with a hearty "Amen."[35]

The death of his brothers forced Walker to place politics
in abeyance and devote most of his time to business and
study. When Jeremiah died, he undertook the settlement
of his estate, but Jeremiah's wife was uneasy over the
arrangement because Walker was in school at the time. To
placate her he took a rash step for a student of twenty and
offered to assume all the debts and credits of the estate and
to pay her $2,000. At first the widow was hesitant but, after
"all her relatives held a long consultation with her," she
agreed. Walker realized that he was giving a certainty for
an uncertainty, but he could find no other means to
"square" his conduct and, at the same time, "please all
parties."

Placed on sale, Jeremiah's slaves brought far more than
Walker had hoped,[36] yet before he knew how much he was
to gain or lose from the liquidation of this estate, he had to
become the principal executor of Memorable's. Memorable's will divided his estate equally between his widow,
Sally B. Walker, and John Williams. Walker was thus
placed in the position of assuming half of his brother's
debts and credits as well as half of his estate, real and
personal. The widow and another brother, Henry Graves,
were also appointed executors, but the real responsibility
and initiative fell to Walker. "H.G.W." was "unacquainted
with many transactions of a mercantile nature," and "sister
S.B.W." disclaimed any participation in the business.[37]

To complicate matters further, Memorable had formed
an agreement with James Sanders in March, 1803. By its
terms James freed himself of all business obligations in
Petersburg so that he could enter business in Augusta;
Memorable assumed James' share of their mercantile busi-

ness in Petersburg, including the firm's obligations, and received James' share of their father's estate.[38] Walker found that Memorable's estate owed numerous and considerable debts, and many were due it, several of long standing and of a disputable nature. "The debts which we owe are sure and certain to be paid by us," he wrote, "whilst on the contrary those due us are subject to a thousand difficulties." Although he was confident that the estate would be sufficient to cover the debts with something left over, he realized it would take careful management to attain this result.[39] Late in the year he devised a plan to terminate the affair satisfactorily. If Sally, his sister-in-law, would agree to "break up" their plantation in the spring, they could sell a large portion of their slaves and with the proceeds pay many of their debts. The mills could then be rented, or they could employ someone to superintend them, and what few Negroes remained could be hired out and the land rented. Sally concurred, and by this means many of the estate's obligations were met in 1804. The two largest payments were made to Walker's future father-in-law, Colonel Pope, who received $3,971.22 ¾ on January 1, and $1,562 somewhat later, the second payment covering successful suits against the firm of Pope and Walker.[40]

Walker's supervision of his brothers' estates burdened him for the better part of two years, yet during this time he was also a student at the Academy of Moses Waddel, located across the river from Petersburg in Vienna, South Carolina. Probably the South of that day could offer no better preparatory education. Waddel had first come to the area in 1794 as a 22-year-old Presbyterian minister. His first school, established near Appling in Columbia County, Georgia, supplied William H. Crawford with the only formal education he ever received. In the next year, Waddel had met and married the sister of one of his pupils, John C. Calhoun. Within a few months his bride was dead, and the grief-stricken Waddel devoted full time to evangelism for a number of years. In 1801, accompanied by a new wife, he opened the Vienna Academy.[41]

Waddel was a superb teacher who chose to teach a primarily classical curriculum. He did his own papergrading and daily heard his scholars recite individually. He whipped his boys for grave violations of discipline, but there were few occasions when such punishment was required. One of his students wrote, "To be 'turned off', as it was called—that is, to have to get a lesson over a second time, was considered such a disgrace by the students, that if this did not cure the fault, whipping, he well knew, would not."[42] The annual spring exhibitions when students were examined by visitors provided additional incentives for hard work. For many years the judges included Dr. W. W. Bibb, Crawford, and Calhoun.[43]

Calhoun, first among many of Waddel's scholars to distinguish themselves in leading Northern universities, was grateful to his former teacher. He wrote that Waddel "may be justly considered as the father of classical education in the upper country of South Carolina and Georgia." He believed the key to Waddel's success lay in "a felicitous combination of qualities for government of boys and communicating to them what he knew, and judged the teacher "particularly successful in exciting emulation among them, and of obtaining the good will of all except the worthless."[44] That Waddel was exceptional is clear from the statement repeatedly made by Dr. Samuel Stanhope Smith, President of Nassau-Hall (Princeton University), who said that he received "no scholars from any section of the United States who stand a better examination than the pupils of Dr. Waddel."[45]

When he could free himself from business, Walker loved "the philosophic ease of academic leisure" at the Academy. He bemoaned the fact that "when one's head is full of notions of business, it becomes totally unfit for study."[46] Yet he kept consistently at his work. On July 4, 1803, he took part in an exhibition at the school and was disappointed that no orations were given in the town of Petersburg, due, he said, to the negligence of the townspeople. When the students left for their vacations immediately thereafter, Walker agreed to hear three local boys recite, among them his future brother-in-law, Willis Pope. He wrote that he did not take them in the hope of getting money, but "to heighten my knowledge in the Latin, and because I esteem them, and their parents."[47]

During the summer Walker made known his decision to study law and began to assess his own qualifications. "I am certain," he wrote, "that I shall never be an eloquent speaker." His voice was not sufficiently strong and he had an "impediment" when speaking which rendered some of his words "unintelligible," yet he determined to prepare himself as best he could and to present himself at the bar. He had always admired a country life, but came to feel that an "uneasiness attended it" which was wanting elsewhere. In the near future, at least, he thought he would be "much better contented" were he "immured in the precincts of a college" than placed over many servants.[48]

From the time of his enrollment at the Academy, Walker had hoped to go to Princeton for a year or two. In the fall of 1803, involved in complicated litigation, he seriously questioned the practicality of his plans, and wondered if he would ever be able to "rise above mediocrity." "I was not formed to grovel in the dust and mud of plebeian humility," he wrote. "I am too ambitious for that. I want to serve my country—and I want to be known hereafter—excuse me if you please, but believe me I wish to be good as well as popular."[49]

Though the pressure of circumstances seemed to dictate that Walker leave school and become a "gentleman farmer," he continued his work at the Waddel Academy. When student orations and two plays highlighted the exhibitions of 1804, Walker contributed a speech on the career of George Washington. He felt he had improved a great deal and succeeded as well as he had any right to hope. "The people could feel the subject if not the eloquence of the orator," he wrote. The audience was most pleased by the stage productions, *The Drummer, or the Haunted House,* and *She Stoops to Conquer, or the Mistakes of a Night.* "Happily for us," Walker concluded, "the people in the backwoods, who generally constitute our audience on these occasions are not very critical judges of dramatic exhibitions, or displays of oratorical powers."[50]

To the best of his opportunity he himself had been an avid patron of the theater for several years. At sixteen, he was overcome by the wonderful artistry of a Mr. Hughes and Mrs. Williamson who had come to Petersburg to perform. They remained an entire theatrical week (six days), presenting such works as *The Provoked Husband* and *The Spoiled Child.* Walker was present at every performance, as was most of Petersburg.

At the Academy, he became a Thespian briefly. After long hours of rehearsal, he looked forward to what he described as his last local appearance. Two days before the event, he was seized by a "very bad cold," which, together with the fact that he "should be in the vocatives on the morrow," affected him so that he could hardly talk. Yet his was the concluding speech, and at its conclusion there was warm applause. "It must have been . . . merely to approve of the exhibition in toto and not my speech individually," he explained.[51]

The experience did not dull his appreciation of the theater, which he felt to be the "most rational, entertaining amusement purchasable by money." He denied that its adverse effect outweighed its beneficial ones, as some of his friends contended, and held that he would always spend whatever amount it might take to get the best seats. When he heard that Fayetteville, North Carolina, had appeared ungenerous in support of a troop of visiting actors, he was appalled. He maintained that one could hardly encourage too much the "genius and wit" of actors, and he did everything possible to further their craft.[52]

Immediately after the 1804 exhibitions, Waddel moved his school from Vienna to his plantation, about five miles beyond. Walker described all the students as "in the vocatives" because of the move. He hoped they would not be "surfeited with the 'sweets of rural life.' " As for himself, he declared that he would follow Waddel anywhere, yet he seemed to have little actual affection for the man. Waddel was an outstanding teacher but a rather cold personality. When he displayed some emotion while conducting the funeral of a mutual friend, Walker confessed, "Mr. Waddel here discovered a warmth of affection of which I scarcely thought him capable."[53]

By the spring of 1805, Walker felt his dream of attending Princeton could come true. "I have just left my good old friend Moses," he wrote, as he prepared for the trip north. At the last moment business conditions again intervened,

but he vowed they would not impede him further. He
would make his "escape on all fools day,"—possibly a
"portent for his future life."[54]

For his time, Walker probably had better than adequate
preparation. In addition to his wide reading and fine
secondary training, he had traveled extensively in his
native state and in South Carolina. His experience as a
deputy post carrier had been particularly broadening,
though initially he had been ill-equipped to perform his
duties. Being entirely a stranger to the country, he had
been frequently lost and often the object of amusement on
his first trip as Memorable's replacement. "I was . . .
gazed at by every gaping huzzy and bumpkin at every house
I passed, whose eyes were fixed in mute astonishment at the
postman team," he declared. Moreover, his horse was lame
and "of a slow and lazy disposition." He felt "Mad as the
maddest of March hares," at the journey's end. On another
occasion, he had taken the wrong road from Edgefield
Courthouse and gone some eighteen miles in the wrong
direction. Yet these trips of over 200 miles had their
compensations, races, balls, and friendly receptions in
gracious homes among them. Riding the post route certainly gave Walker a more extensive knowledge of others
than most of his neighbors ever received.[55]

In truth it was no country bumpkin who left provincial
Georgia for Princeton in April, 1805. By disposition,
intellect, and training, John Williams Walker had every
right to look forward to success.

FOUR

A Swing Around the Circle

SO EXTENDED A JOURNEY NORTH AS THE TRIP FROM PETERS-
burg to Princeton proffered fascinating new experiences
to a young man with keen perceptions. Walker traveled by
stage coach, taking a route which included stops at Salem,
N.C., Richmond, Washington, Philadelphia and Baltimore.
The day had not yet arrived when all American cities
seemed cut to a uniform pattern, and consequently great
variety enlivened the descriptions Walker wrote in his
letters. The exhilarating new sights, the new sensations,
were shared by fellow travelers in the coach, all of whom,
regrettably, found the early part of the journey unattrac-
tive. "Had not the Salada, Broad, and Cahaba rivers rolled
their waters across our route, Nature would not have appeared altogether lovely to us." Indeed they often saw for
miles nothing but "smoky tents to cheer their fatigue."

But at Salem, they found "a considerable town" in-
habited by the United Brotherhood and "situated in a
country which for many miles contains none but Dutch
[German Moravians]." The town itself was very agreeable,
containing many good houses of brick, and the people
were, in Walker's opinion, the "very counterpart of everything that is clean, prepossessing or lovely." Nevertheless,
no one was as well clad as the travelers themselves, and the

people's manners were frequently crude. Walker's group attended church services with about 200 of the "Brethren" of both sexes. There, the preacher alternated between singing with the organ and delivering his sermon—using "Dutch," which, according to Walker, reduced to a minimum the "evangelical advantages" reaped by the travelers. The Moravian ladies kept their heads continually bowed during the services.[1]

North Carolina was noteworthy for its poor roads and barren countryside without so much as a fine tree for a hundred miles. In Virginia, too, the landscape had a melancholy tone because of the many "old fields" which had "become a distinguishing and characteristic trait of the country." The effect was counteracted, however, by the "large and elegant houses where the hospitable gentlemen of 'the ancient dominion' live in state." Hospitality did not, unfortunately, extend to the state's innkeepers, who, the travelers found, demanded exorbitant prices for indifferent services.[2]

Walker had mixed reactions to Richmond. The armory was large and convenient, the Capitol elegant—even magnificent. The James Canal, main channel of the city's commerce, ran for seven or eight miles along the north side of the James River, terminating in a two- or three-acre basin which was harbor for innumerable boats transporting flour, coal, and other products. The canal greatly facilitated the city's business, even though shallow rapids made access to the basin impossible for large vessels. These had to dock at wharves about a mile below the city.

Though he was greatly impressed with the bustling commercial life, Walker deplored Richmond society. Richmond citizens were preoccupied with making money, he declared, and on departure he recorded the fact that he had spent few days in any society which pleased him less. There was one outstanding memory—that of the full-length statue of George Washington. He confessed that he looked at it "with more satisfaction than the spacious structure in which it is placed," and described his "reverential awe" as "alone and unobserved" he paced the room in which the statue stood "elevated on a marble pedestal . . . protected from the . . . intruder by a railing of iron."[3]

Arriving in Washington, D.C., Walker and his companions discovered much to admire. The Capitol was "beyond comparison, the most magnificent structure" his eyes had ever beheld. The Senate chamber particularly impressed him, the pictures of a number of illustrious men hanging against the walls rendering it "aweful in perspective." In its turn, Baltimore was a beautiful city, but "by suffering the merchants to lead the water to too great a distance up the streets," the people had perhaps made it unhealthy. Again he observed an all-pervasive air of commerce.

When Walker reached Philadelphia, a beautiful new bridge over the Schuylkill was the pride of the town. He had determined to stay for a few days here, and the added time gave him the opportunity to visit the city's museum, where he viewed the wonders with amazement. As for the city itself, he found it much larger than Baltimore, with many convenient and spacious houses, few of which had either "elegance or magnificence." Not a single street was as well built as Baltimore's Market Street. He expressed some doubt that after seeing all these exhilarating sights he would ever be able to settle down to study.[4]

In Delaware, nature seemed to be "more modest and regular" than in Georgia. The meadows were green, the finest orchards were in bloom and the farms in the highest state of cultivation. "And yet," Walker wrote, "the country is not so romantic and picturesque as more to the South . . . and altho the view of a vast level plain, interspersed with fruits and extensive fields of wheat . . . may fill us with ideas of beauty; yet it is to mountains and precipices we must look for sublimity and terrour [sic]."[5]

The Princeton which was journey's end for Walker was, in 1805, one of America's leading institutions of higher learning, although it had fewer than 200 students. The campus was new, a fire in 1802 having destroyed the college building and along with it all but 100 of the library's 3,000 volumes and most of the students' belongings. Within a matter of weeks, rebuilding had gotten under way, using as a base the walls which had been left standing. Now, two new buildings, Stanhope Hall and the Philosophical Building (which curiously enough housed the kitchen and dining-hall as well as the philosophical apparatus room, mathematics and natural philosophy classrooms and an observatory), were completed and in use. Stanhope Hall held the library, study halls, rooms for the literary societies, and presidential recitation rooms.

President Samuel Stanhope Smith led a faculty of four professors and two tutors. Dr. Smith, reputed to be a century ahead of his time in educational theory, had seen many of his proposals stifled by a conservative board of trustees which looked upon the school as an indoctrination center for Presbyterianism. To the president's revolutionary proposal that the study of classical languages be replaced with modern foreign languages in classes above the freshman level, the trustees returned an unqualified "No." They employed students to spy on both president and faculty, and scanned all scholarly papers with suspicious, reactionary eyes.

Dr. Smith had recovered from tuberculosis. Never a strong man physically, he was either unable or unwilling to fight with great vigor for the innovations he would like to have made. He had been highly successful as leader of the fund-raising campaign which followed the fire, and as a result, largely, of his efforts, Princeton emerged from the disaster with greater prestige and more students than it had had previously. He was also at least partially successful in his attempts to widen the scope of instruction in the sciences. He had purchased equipment to be used in the astronomy, physics, and chemistry classes, and had engaged a Scottish chemist, John McClean, to teach the physical sciences. The historian of Princeton has observed that McClean's courses in these fields "excited the keen interest of the students but his experiments in chemistry, said to be the first made in any American college, were the wonder of Nassau Hall."[6]

Walker enjoyed good health during his first summer of residence, "unless a headache and sometimes an ephemeral diarrhea" be considered. He devoted most of his time to study, and quarterly examinations prevented him from writing his brothers and friends for some time. Having finished these, he took up "Viscesimus Knox on Education" and became so absorbed in it that he could not put it down until he had gone through the system. In the fall he devoted part of his vacation to studying history and geography, but he still found time to divert himself occasionally with "the private conversations of Pope and Swift." This, he explained, was one innocent amusement which would prevent one from sinking into vice.[7] Despite such diversions, Walker and his classmates led a fairly dull life at Princeton. Affluence had unfortunately brought the college less inspiring teachers, and some were "poor dis-

ciplinarians." Gathering with professors for informal dis-
cussions, a stimulating feature of Princeton life in earlier
years, was no longer customary. A typical day for an
upperclassman was, though dull, nonetheless far from lazy.
It began with morning prayers at 6:00, continued with
study until breakfast at 7:30; then there was study until
2:00, interrupted only by lunch. From 2:00 to 5:00 recita-
tions were heard; supper was at 6:00, and afterwards study
again. At 9:00, tutors checked the rooms to see that all
students were in. Princeton's only recreation was conversation and perhaps a walk after supper. Students were given
no voice in undergraduate affairs, and for the most part
their minds " 'bogged down' under the succession of written lectures, memory exercises, and quizzes, and their
schedules were quite a physical strain. . . ."[8]

As he became acclimated to the routine, Walker came to
love the life at Princeton. He boasted of his landlady's good
food, his jovial companions, and the abundance of books.
He was contented, he said, but not happy. He also boasted
a new humility. "I see my own comparative insignificance. . . . I see that 'pride is not made for man.' "
Distinction, whether in war, politics or letters, was not
easily attained, and its anticipated joys vanished upon its
possession. Man must be wise who "traces the path marked
out by nature" and is not swayed by the pressure of
ambition. Nevertheless he was forced to admit in more
sincere moments that he did not, indeed, despise the
honors which his fellow countrymen could confer upon
him. "I reverence, I adore my Country," he wrote; "its
honors are worthy of labors, and dangers, and sufferings. I
am unfit, I am unworthy to wear them." There were men
at Princeton, contemporaries of Walker himself, who were
capable of holding, in his opinion, the reins of govern-

ment; he only hoped that "their virtues [would] keep pace with their abilities."[9]

Epidemics of fever prevented Walker from visiting Philadelphia and New York during the fall vacation of 1805. His good friend Larkin Newby paid a short visit to Princeton—which was some compensation—but after he left, Walker was gripped by loneliness. He "mope[d] about the streets of Princeton, or pore[d] over the pages of some English Classic" until the semester convened. "Senior" Walker now decided to board outside the college, even though he had to take accommodations rather too far from the recitation rooms and at greater expense. He found the new arrangements expedient since here he was "absolute master" of his own time and was not obliged "to be *bored* by every idle fellow who professes to respect me." His new quarters proved especially valuable during the winter months when the snow prevented many outdoor pastimes and "the spirit of visiting" was "much more prevalent than in summer."[10]

Walker was scarcely situated in his new abode when he became ill. For four weeks he was plagued with an extremely bad cold, coughing, and headaches. At length he was able to resume his school work, but he never again enjoyed robust health, and very probably he was afflicted with tuberculosis from this time on.[11] Fortunately, the season was temperate. As late as November 23 no snow had yet fallen, and Walker "experienced no change between this and our Georgia winter." Somewhat later in the year sleighing and skating would be the chief outdoor amusements.[12]

His poor health and concentration on study, however, did not divorce him completely from all extra-curricular activities. He sought out convivial entertainment, although he abominated large parties "where there is no static amusement proposed," finding them ruinous to conversation. "A significant nod comprehends the *ne plus ultra* of what is said and done,"[13] he wrote of such gatherings. These were not for him. Spending three hours with a "parcel of—girls" was more in his line.

Walker had planned to make an Eastern tour in the summer of 1806, but the friends who promised to accompany him had to withdraw. Since he felt a private trip of this extent would delete his funds too seriously, he gave up the idea and went only to New York and Philadelphia. He found the theater diverting, and, although he saw "no Cooper, nor Fennel," he was well entertained by "Jefferson & Wood & Harwood and Mrs. W. Guell." Concerts by Mrs. Jones and Mrs. Woodham added variety.[14]

But nothing could keep Walker's mind from thoughts of Matty Pope for very long. When he learned that she had returned from the North, he wrote that the needle of his affection again had swung "toward the sultry regions of the South." He urged his brother, James Sanders, to tell him what he thought of her. Had she changed? Had her intellect matured? Was she "free from the violence of anger, the meanness of revenge, the pride of riches, the egotism of vanity, or the influences of a shrew?" And, above all, was she still fond of him? A separation of two years had not served to allay "the effervescence of youthful blood." Was the choice of his boyhood still valid?[15] When James Sanders replied that Matty had retained all her finest qualities, Walker importuned for more information. He wondered if she were still handsome. He did not ask that she be beautiful. "God forbid!" he wrote. "If she were, she would, almost to a certainty, be vain and haughty; & then I should gravely put my hat under my arm, make her a formal (or, if you please, a pedantic) bow, and so bid her ladyship an eternal farewell."[16]

Had Matty developed an interest in literary subjects? He hoped that she had found something to amuse a cultivated mind, "something more pleasing . . . than the perpetual round of thimble selling and pawn-paying riddles & kisses." She had read a good deal, he knew, especially "in the novel line," and he wondered if it had polished her intercourse with others.[17]

Even now, Walker's love was still undeclared. He did not know whether Matty would cast so much as a lingering glance at him. At times, with fear gripping his heart, he tried to prepare for the worst, as when he wrote Newby[18] in June that he had no marks or expressions of her love, and that he would not "pop" his head into a "furnace to save the eighteenth of her finger or her little toenail. I shall not," he declared, "spend my life in building a ladder to the moon . . . in one word Confound me if I will love any woman who will not love me."

As his graduation approached, Walker grew moody. His life was being spent "in mere procrastination" without distinction or credit to anyone. He felt himself to be "an isolated individual" with neither mother nor father nor scarcely anyone else to serve as a stimulus. He realized, he said, how little he knew, and how brief was the span of human life which largely "precludes any great addition" to the reservoir of knowledge. "I feel, not without regret, that I was born but to eat, and die, and rot, and be forgotten—that fifty years in probability there will be no momento [sic] that such an animal [as myself] ever existed."[19]

In the fall of 1806 he was graduated with distinction, and prepared to leave Princeton with both grief and joy. "I found something in Princeton," he wrote to his brother, that "I had never found before, and perhaps shall never find again. . . . I found more warmth and friendship and cordiality than I expected, and my feelings were more intense accordingly."[20] Shortly after enrolling he had expressed the hope only that he might acquire a knowledge "of those branches of science which daily employ our attention" and might "maintain a respectable standing" in his class, disclaiming any intention of obtaining honors. In these aspirations he was eminently successful.[21] As long as he lived he was to be grateful for the additional training gained at Princeton.

He was forced to pay, just before setting out for Petersburg, what he called "a not inconsiderable sum" for "a friend whose surety" he had undertaken. Left with funds only sufficient to take him to Washington, the stranded young man wrote James Sanders for money on which to come home. He also directed Henry Graves, apparently the custodian of his affairs in Petersburg, to repay James at once. Once in Washington, however, he revived an old plan to remain there for a few months, hearing the "great little men" and the "little great men" set forth their "interested patriotism and personal antipathy," reading newspapers and "western conspiracies," and attending balls, whist parties and "tea conventions."[22] Forever introspective, he began to think himself "too indolent and slow and indecisive for anything truly useful or great." He could not serve others for attending to himself.[23] At the same time he was confident that his own talents were superior to those of many members of the Congress. "I wish to God the carpet were taken from the Representative Chamber so that such goats as Sloan and My Lord James Holland & some half a score others might be *scraped* into silence whenever they presumed to trouble the house with their 'retrospective backward' & all such stuff," he wrote. That the purse of the nation could be "lightened by those eternal babblers: none of whom can talk grammar or commonsense to save them from perdition," seemed to him insufferable. He was sorry that the stenographer corrected their usage, because the people should see uncensored a demonstration of the talents of their leaders. Only the speeches of John Randolph suffered in the secretary's box, and these lost something of magnificence and incisiveness when retouched by the grammarians.

Yet Walker's reason taught him that distance had added stature to many of the leaders he now saw in close proximity. He had come to Washington with high expectations, "prepared to idolize the Solomons of the land—to see eloquence exert its force—to see gentlemen & scholars & statesmen agitate the greatest matters of the greatest empire on earth." He had come "to hear all the beauty of language and the wisdom of intellect." Now, he found "Solomons are very few, and there is not more than one Chatham among them."[24] His disillusionment upon close sight was natural, he knew. "No one," he wrote "can be a hero to his *valet-de-chambre.*"

Depressed in spirits, Walker was eager to leave Washington, and had made plans to ride back to Georgia with Dr. W. W. Bibb, now a Congressman, in early March, 1807. But once more he was attacked by what he called a cold and fever, and his illness prevented him from undertaking an overland journey. "I must ride about considerably and exercise myself next summer to brace my nerves and re-establish my declining health," he wrote, at the same time refusing to complain, because complaints should be left to "grannies and unsuccessful lovers."[25] A sea voyage seemed to promise improvement in his health, and he struggled with arrangements, plagued by a dozen disappointments at once. The time of the departure of his ship from Baltimore was changed again and again, as was the place of its destination. Then there were delays waiting for sailors "who must first expend their wages in the grog shop" before coming aboard. "We talk of sailing tomorrow and the next day," said Walker, "but it is an hundred to one that we hear the Sunday Sermon bell and take the prayer of the Church with us."[26]

The wind staged further delays. Then the ship finally set sail and, to Walker's dismay, arrived in Philadelphia. After waiting ten days he was "hundreds of miles toward the north pole" instead of closer to Petersburg. On the advice of a doctor he rejected passage on "a dirty little schooner" bound for Charleston, returning instead to Baltimore, where more acceptable transportation to the same city was available. His attempts to get home had proved so expensive that he was forced to borrow $50 from a Philadelphia merchant, Richard Lunis. "A man can neither travel nor be sick without paying for it," he found.[27] At the same time his heart beat "high with the thoughts of home."[28]

But once in Petersburg Walker did not find the health and contentment he sought. Through the long summer he waited for his illness and dejection to disperse. The fever wrote "a receipt in full" upon his lips, and his cough abated somewhat, yet he remained "as dull and melancholy as ever." At times he thought of himself "with sort of mingled wonder and indignation"; once "all animation, vivacity and frolic," he was now "dum, downhearted, and half dead with the hypocondriac [sic]." In late February,

1808, still suffering melancholia, he decided to resume his travels, this time choosing to go southwest as he sought for peace and health.

Walked reached Savannah on February 29 "half dead with fatigue, a bone cracked in every foot." At the theater here he encountered two or three Princeton friends who had "not yet lost all Princeton feeling," and who temporarily dispelled his gloom.[29] The weather was pleasant, and he lingered in Savannah for several days before moving on to Charleston, a city suffering from the embargo. Business was dull, and the "poor sailors" were "flying to the country for subsistence."[30] Though less than a month had passed, he found cause for poignant suffering in his separation from Matty Pope. He wrote his brother that he had bade her farewell "in the language of my heart before I leave the land perhaps forever." He hoped that God would bless his loved ones in Petersburg "with abundance of health and happiness," and trusted he was not saying goodbye to them, "for ever."[31]

By late April, he was in New Orleans—at best a great disappointment to him. Not to be found here was "that spiry grandeur" of architecture which distinguished the cities of the North. Everything in New Orleans "is humble and common," he wrote, explaining that hurricanes sometimes lifted the river above its banks, and made it necessary to build houses low for safety. The principal buildings, "a Catholic Cathedral, a town-hall, a government-house and an old wooden dingy Hospital," he thought unimpressive. The government had just sent from Washington materials for a customhouse. Of the two forts, one was in good repair and garrisoned by two companies of troops. The other, demilitarized earlier, had been fortified during the Burr panic by General Wilkinson, but by the time of Walker's visit it was again abandoned.

Despite the embargo, the New Orleans harbor was active. Walker attributed the "considerable quantity of shipping" to the city's extensive coastal trade, which made the restrictions "fall as lightly on New Orleans as any port in the Union." Nonetheless, large numbers of Kentucky boats with cargoes of hams and potatoes were tied up, "rotting at the levee"—mute testimony to the embargo's toll.

Worthy of lengthy comment in a letter to Newby were the city's nuns. Walker wrote that there were women here who for all he knew "may have blood in their veins and wishes in their hearts," yet "had almost as well been formed of sticks and stones, for they shut themselves from the world and all its pleasure." He could never believe that "the beneficent God" accepts with favor "a mode of worship which if universal would soon leave him without worshippers." There was no doubt, however, that the nuns were "sincere tho' misguided devotees, and pure as the icicle of which they are the emblem."[32]

New Orleans proffered "little of [the] grand or beautiful to solicit praise." The houses were discolored like those in Charleston; the two little French theaters were not worth mentioning, and the few newspapers were poor. On April 30, the anniversary of the cession of Louisiana, the flag of every ship in the harbor streamed in the wind, but Walker took no pleasure in the celebration. Time and the embargo had cut down the size of the fete, but even so the clang of bells and boom of cannon were nearly constant throughout the day. Walker was contemptuous. "A fine way of demonstrating joy and paying honors to distract a whole town with headaches and beat the tatoo [sic] of a bottle on the drum of its ears."

In all probability he looked on everything he saw with the jaundice of poor health and loneliness. The people for whom he had a letter of introduction were absent from the "strange, foreign-tongued city." He walked the streets, looked at the girls, visited the Exchange, saw a French play, and lived "in hopes of a quadroon ball." In his lodgings, the landlady's daughter was neither beautiful nor charming, while the landlady herself possessed a "pair of legs of the circumference of Falstaff's belly."[33] Ill as he was, he began to plan his return to Georgia, but before leaving he decided to go into the Mississippi Territory for what he thought would be a brief "inspection trip." The excursion changed his entire future. In Washington, the little town chosen in 1802 as the capital of the infant Territory, Walker met Thomas Percy, a Princeton classmate and a man to whom he gave "as much love" as to a brother. Percy insisted that his friend remain with him for a time, and Walker consented.[34]

A strange combination of wealth and poverty, culture and crudity, characterized the Natchez region. Though Washington was the new capital, it was Natchez, six miles away, that was flourishing. Built on the summit of hills 100 feet above the river, the city had some 3,000 people, nearly 300 dwellings, and two newspapers. Shortly after the turn of the century, Mexican cotton had been found to be the variety best suited for the area, and its extensive cultivation had increased the price of improved lands near the town to an average of $20 an acre. Week in and week out a mile-long column of boats lined the lower bank of the river. There was a distinct flavor of the frontier. None of the streets or sidewalks was paved, and skins of cougars which had been killed in the adjacent country served a number of stores as doors. Gangs of idle Indians—Choctaw, Natchez, Muskogee—strolled about, and across the river wild horses herded within easy sight of the town. Transportation except by water continued to be very difficult, even though the federal government had ordered the Natchez Trace widened to sixteen feet as far north as Nashville. In 1808, however, long stretches of the Trace were still impassable except by packhorse. Only the year before, the "Three Chopped Way" had been marked overland through Fort Stoddert to Milledgeville.[35]

Washington, on the other hand, "enjoyed some reputation as the 'Versailles' of the territory" because of the brilliance of its social life. Politics had seemingly dictated its choice as capital, for it was "supposedly far enough removed to be safe from the influence of the wealthy classes"—presumed to be Federalists. Nevertheless, Natchez was so close that there was never any real separation between the people of the two towns.[36]

At first Walker planned to spend only the summer with his friends, but in the end he lingered until May, 1809. The Percys were well-to-do planters who led a very pleasant life; he was devoted to Thomas Percy, who served him in the place of "relations, and friends, and home and almost of Love"; and it was his great good fortune to be in the care of one of the nation's outstanding physicians, Dr. Samuel Brown.[37]

The 39-year-old Brown, one-time pupil of Dr. Benjamin Rush, had attended the University of Edinburgh and, after further study at Marischal College, University of Aberdeen, had returned to America with a prestigious medical degree. After practicing successfully for a brief time, he accepted a post as professor of chemistry, anatomy, and surgery in the new medical curriculum at Transylvania University, Kentucky. One of his biographers has emphasized his versatility.

> He was one of the most progressive men of his day, not only in medical lines, but also in other walks of life. He was probably the first American to make known to his countrymen the discovery of the art of lithography in Europe and suggested places in Kentucky where suitable stone for the purpose could be procured. He first suggested the method of clarifying ginseng for the Chinese market. He also originated the idea for the use of steam instead of direct heat in the distillation of spirits, and introduced into the United States the use of lithotrity [an operation in which stones in the bladder are broken into pieces small enough to be voided] soon after its first application by French surgeons. He was a pioneer in the inoculation for smallpox, and had vaccinated upwards of five hundred persons in Lexington by 1802.[38]

In recognition of his achievements, Dr. Brown had been made a member of the American Philosophical Society in 1800, probably through the influence of Dr. Rush and Thomas Jefferson.[39]

Walker and Dr. Brown joined the Percy circle at about the same time—Dr. Brown because he fell in love with and married Thomas' sister, Catherine Percy. He settled on a neighboring plantation, giving up the practice of medicine "except for occasional calls to his sick friends and gratuitous attention to the neighboring poor." Walker was soon numbered chief among his sick friends, and with the doctor's constant and expert care, the young man began to improve. By October he was already able to ride at full gallop and walk up a hill without resting.[40] But the dejection of illness often returned. He began to "feel the winter" early. He heard nothing from Georgia. "I have no letters to reply to, for my friends seem to have abandoned me in silence to the sadness of my exile. Solitude & Silence are worse than Consumption himself," he wrote.[41] He resolved to remain "an idle careless fellow," a resolve quite unlike any he had made a few months before. "I have already seen the ruin of my best hopes; my aspirations after greatness and fame have perished like the dream of a feverish man," he said. "I am content to walk my little hour upon the stage, to die, to rot, and be forgotten like the common mass of mankind that fall around me every day unheeded and unlamented." In the meanwhile, he would enjoy friendships and the simpler pleasures to the fullest extent.[42]

He was amused by a group of "Natchez bucks and idlers" who formed themselves into a Thespian band and presented two plays in Washington. He had heard rumors that the Charleston company of players had spent the summer in Augusta, and he caught himself wondering if any of the Petersburg ladies had been seen in his brothers' boxes, or if they were "all dead or married."[43]

Earlier in the year Walker had written Henry Graves to sell his cotton for whatever the market would bear. In February, he urged his brother to have $500 in New Orleans by March 1, 1809, for his return trip.[44] He had seen the Near West, had made progress in recovering his health and spirits, and had nourished old friendships and founded others; now he was ready for departure.

But not for good. The Mississippi Territory had so impressed him that he had resolved to dispose of his Georgia property and settle where he had found "hospitality and health," and where he hoped to find "independence and wealth." He recorded that the Territory soil was "exceedingly fertile and productive, beyond all comparison superior to that of Georgia." The staple of its cotton was better and ranked higher in foreign prices. Its planters were "rich and hospitable" and many set "sumptuous tables." Yet "everything is dear, merchandize in particular," with Natchez merchants charging "from 50 to 100 [percent] more than the back-wood merchants of the Southern states." At the same time, they extended long term credits. The Territory's climate was a little milder than that of Georgia, though in 1808-1809 when Walker was in Washington the New Year was followed by snow which lay for several days on the ground, and the winter was unusually severe.[45] All things considered, he could not help but look with favor upon the Territory. "I ought to give thanks on my marrow-bones that I was allowed to make a jaunt to this country instead of that strange out-landed *terra incognita,* where there is an everlasting embargo on the export of Ghosts," he wrote. Though his health seemed to be improving, he believed that he would have to "relinquish deep continued study. So the Law may go to the d————l for me: I shall never finger a fee nor put on the ermine robe of office," he declared.[46] He could scarcely have wandered farther from the truth.

In spite of plans to leave in March, it was late May before he moved on to New Orleans, where he was forced to wait three weeks for passage to Charleston. Percy joined him for a week, and the two had long conversations over the possibility of uniting their slaves in a common agricultural endeavor. Without success, Walker tried to persuade Percy to come East with him now, and he was saddened by his failure.[47] He could not foresee that within a few years Percy and Dr. Brown and his children would join him in a trek to Alabama.[48]

As the New Orleans heat increased and possibilities of direct transport to Charleston became more remote, Walker abandoned the attempt to find it and accepted passage much farther north. On June 22, his ship docked at Trenton, New Jersey. It had been scheduled for Philadelphia, but the presence on board of "one or two devils shaking with the ague," together with the fact that the vessel was out of New Orleans led the board of health to condemn her to quarantine for "lord knows how long." To escape, she moved on to New Jersey, and as a result Walker had a chance to visit Princeton for a day or two.[49]

He returned by water to Charleston and en route to Savannah suffered a hemorrhage. "An old leaky vessel of mine gave way and discharged such quantities of blood as to oblige me to take shelter in a neighboring house," he wrote.[50] He then returned to Charleston, boarded another ship, only to have her meet with obstinate winds which confined the vessel within the bar. Worn out, Walker took land passage home, arriving in Augusta August 21 and in Petersburg shortly thereafter.

In Petersburg he found life looked much the same. The trees were larger, and "some of the girls, being married are bigger—and some unmarried ones are older and uglier and thinner, pining away . . . of celibacy." By late October his health was "pretty much as usual: neither the most desperate, nor yet very flattering." Since his arrival he had ruptured another "crazy blood-vessel," but it was a mere trifle compared to the Charleston hemorrhage. He was disgusted, however, by being "effectually embargoed here this winter, perhaps for life." The West was out of the question since his health was poor and he "could hardly *give* away any land now," it was so little in demand. He felt "compelled to remain" until he could sell his holdings. He prayed that "consumption and the climate may be good natured and take pity on a poor miserable devil of a wight who is unable to run away from them and who throws himself upon their clemency and forbearance."[51]

FIVE

The Formative Period

IN VIEW OF THE DESPONDENCY EXPRESSED IN HIS LETTER TO
Newby of October 25, 1809, and the apparent hopelessness
with which Walker looked upon his plans for moving West,
the events which occurred in the next three months are
astonishing. In this brief time John Williams Walker had
not only completed plans to move to Madison County in
the Mississippi Territory, but had courted, won, and married Matilda Pope. The wedding took place January 30,
1810, with the groom transformed by what he described
to Dr. Brown a little later as "returning health."[1] As might
be expected, there is a considerable hiatus in the constant
stream of personal letters which up to this time had poured
forth from Walker's pen.

Six months earlier, in August 1809, the United States
government had offered Madison County lands for sale for
the first time, the sale taking place in Nashville. Madison
County, the first erected in what is now northern Alabama,
embraced an area in "the great bend" of the Tennessee
River. Perhaps enticed by reports of fertile lands, planters
of the Carolinas, Georgia, Virginia, and Tennessee responded to the sale in great numbers, among them seven
Georgians from the Broad River area—Walker, Colonel
LeRoy Pope, James Manning, Robert Thompson, Peyton

Cox, and Thomas and William Wyatt Bibb—the seven buying what has been estimated as almost one-half of the Madison County lands sold at that time. The average purchaser paid $2.00 an acre, with the government offering an eight per cent discount for cash, and charging six per cent per annum if credit were asked.[2] The planters who invested, for the most part wealthy by early nineteenth century standards, would constitute a new type of settler for the Tennessee Valley.

Walker purchased two quarter-sections in the Nashville sale. To this he added another quarter-section in 1810, and another in 1811, 1812, and 1814. In 1818 he bought from Waddy Tate for $10,000 four quarter-sections in township 2, range 1. Four years later he gave 6,000 pounds of top grade seed cotton for another quarter-section in range 2.[3]

In early June, 1810, the newly-married Walkers, the Pope family, and a number of others undertook the trek to Madison County. Although no record of the route they took is extant, it is probable that they followed the Georgia Road, which ran from Athens to Nashville, to a point near Winchester, Tennessee, and then came down the "Great South Trail" to the bend of the Tennessee. (The direct route across Sand Mountain, the "Georgia State Road," was not completed and opened until several months later.) Certainly the trip was not an easy one, but it must have had its rewards. A few years later Gideon Lincecum, an early traveler through the territory, recorded his first impressions of the Alabama country in his autobiography. All was "wilderness," he wrote, "full of deer and turkeys and the streams were full of fish." He and his brother flanked the wagons and killed animals and game by day and were equally successful at fishing by night. "We were six weeks on the road," he said, "and, altogether it was, as I thought and felt, the most delightful time I had ever spent in my life."[4]

Walker and Matilda settled some eight miles north of Hunt's Spring in a log cabin home. They gave it the name of Oakland, but even thus glorified to plantation status, it must have seemed a rude host for Matilda's prized furniture and fine china, forwarded to her by James Sanders in the spring of 1811.[5] No inconvenience, however, could have dampened the Walkers' ardor for the new country. Walker felt it was "the handsomest" he had ever seen.[6] Madison County, a bare two years old when they arrived, seemed particularly fortunate in its topography. Rolling uplands gradually leveled off to a wide valley with a temperate and agreeable climate and a soil capable of yielding "10 barrels of corn or 1000 pounds of cotton" to the acre. Its only drawback was the difficulty of transporting goods to market.[7] When the abundant rains of winter made it possible to navigate the Muscle Shoals, the Valley obtained an outlet to the Mississippi River and the New Orleans market. Otherwise, there were only overland routes to the East, much too expensive to permit the successful sale of cotton in the Savannah, Augusta, or Charleston markets.

Primitive as their life must have been at first, it was a far cry from that of the earlier settlers in the region. The Walkers enjoyed not only necessities but luxuries brought overland, shipped from Augusta by James Sanders, who also served as Walker's agent in Georgia.[8] Coffee and sugar, soap and "groceries," arrived by wagon to ease their situation. Less than five years earlier, Madison countians had been forced to rely heavily on hominy as a staple of diet, since there were no mills in the area to convert corn into meal and transportation was so costly and toilsome.

Wheat flour had not even appeared in the Valley until the population had risen into the thousands. Then it was brought down the Tennessee on flatboats to Ditto's Landing, and at length overland to Hunt's Spring. Game furnished wild meat in abundance, but salt was a precious commodity which had to be imported, and gunpowder to supply the flintlock rifle—the indispensable weapon of the wilderness—had to be laboriously manufactured from sulphur, saltpeter, and charcoal made from willow wood. Iron was so scarce that many a cabin was built without using a trace of it. A triangle in the center of an Indian world, Madison County was cleared by men dressed in buckskin and homespun shirts, men who never owned a foot of the land they tilled and who apparently still felt they had found a haven.[9] By 1809, when the laws of the Territory were extended over the County, its pioneer period had ended, and there were some 5,000 people inhabiting it.[10]

The delight Walker took in his new home is evident in his peremptory refusal to leave it despite James Sanders' urging. Prompted by the West Florida revolt of 1810, which cleared the lower Mississippi of Spanish control, James wrote that for the sake of convenience and the hope of profit, the Walkers should move to the lower Mississippi. He was concerned for them and also for Polly Coleman, their sister, now widowed. Shortly after moving to Madison County, Coleman had died, leaving Polly, their children, and a number of slaves in the care of John Williams, who remained their guardian for the rest of his life. Unsuccessful in promoting the move, James Sanders took two of the Coleman boys to teach them the mercantile business.[11]

By far the largest planter and the wealthiest capitalist in the County in the early years was Colonel Pope, Walker's father-in-law. At the 1809 land sales, Pope and two associates had acquired at $23 an acre the quarter-section of land at Hunt's Spring. Some two or three hundred people lived near the Spring, within the present city limits of Huntsville, and it was this site which the Territorial Legislature's commissioners chose for the County seat. The town was laid out under the Mississippi law in 1810, and Walker represented Colonel Pope in the sale of thirty acres of land to the commissioners at approximately their purchase price. Pope's obligations *pro bono publico* dispatched, Walker was empowered to offer the remaining Pope land to the public at a handsome profit to the owner.[12] The new town was at first called Twickenham after the English home of Alexander Pope, but in 1811 the name was changed to Huntsville.

To add to Walker's general euphoria, Matty gave birth to a daughter toward the end of their first year in Madison County. Mary Jane, born December 2, 1810, was "from the hour of birth the most interesting child you have ever seen—fascinating, intelliegent, and beautiful," her father wrote.[13] She proved to be his only daughter.

Despite his protestations that he must relinquish all hope of becoming a lawyer, Walker had read law with diligence and persistence for years. In the fall of 1810, Judge Obediah Jones convened Madison County's first Superior Court of Law and Equity, and at the opening session Walker was licensed to practice. Edward C. Betts, one of the early historians of Huntsville, writes that "of the brilliant and promising young lawyers of Huntsville who rose to eminence, he was the most talented and popular."[14] As attorney for the Territory in October, 1811, he obtained six true bills in eight cases before a grand jury.[15] But no advocate is always successful. In 1812, he defended one Eli Newman, charged with the razor murder of Joseph Tetrick.

On Wednesday, December 2 (Mary Jane Walker's second birthday), the jury returned a verdict of guilty, and Walker petitioned Judge Jones for a new trial. On Thursday his motion was denied, and Newman was sentenced to be hanged on Saturday. The hanging occurred as scheduled. Thomas Taylor comments in his "Early History of Madison County" that the speed in which justice was meted out in this case explains the absence of lynchings in the Territory.[16] There is no indication that Walker felt any qualms over the rugged nature of territorial justice, yet one wonders. For the most trivial offenses a frequent sentence was "thirty-nine lashes on the bare back," and forgery was punishable by death. Negroes were often subjected to the cruelest kinds of physical punishments.[17]

Walker's initial venture into politics was hardly propitious. Encouraged by a desire to see his Natchez friends again, he entered the race for the Mississippi Territorial Legislature in May, 1811. Six candidates vied for the three positions, and Walker was one of the three defeated. The election of Gabriel Moore, the tax assessor, Colonel Peter Perkins, commander of the militia, and Hugh McVay, an early settler and a justice of the peace, reflected the dominance Tennesseans held over the County—a dominance undiminished until 1817. Walker took solace in the fact that he was "a stranger" to many settlers, and contended that his defeat was accomplished by the "art and intrigue and low cunning and lying set to work" against him. He vowed it would "be the last time" that he would "be a candidate for popular favor."[18] But a scarce two months later on July 4, he was the principal speaker at the militia musters in Huntsville, and his speech had an unmistakable political ring. He praised the New Territory, castigated those who did not wish to defend the Union, and told his audience what they had come to hear. "Where shall we look for so new a country settled like this?" he asked.

It is not two years since the American citizen could legally fix his habitation here; yet look at the population, how numerous, how decent, how opulent, how respectable! It is not merely a rude frontier, thinly peopled with hunters and herdsmen, the mere precursors of the tillers of the earth, but it is the tillers of the earth themselves, who bring with them the pleasures of social life, the arts of industry, the abundant means of easy and comfortable subsistence; and what is better than all this, they bring with them the feelings of independence and Americanism.

Holy God! And is my country to be thus cut off in the very bud and blossom of her glory? . . . Preserve us from the death of suicide. Save me and mine from the deep damnation of sharing in a guilt like this. Cursed be he who lifts up his treasonable voice against this Union; thrice cursed be he who arrays embattled legions against it.[19]

Walker's brother, James Sanders, urged politics upon him with persistence and complete confidence in his eventual success. If Walker would return to Georgia and settle in Athens, which was "the most eligible stand in a Geographical point of view,"[20] he wrote in 1812, he could try for Georgia's sixth seat in the House of Representatives. But no such prospects could have enticed Walker from his new home, the more especially after his two closest friends, Tom Percy and Dr. Samuel Brown, joined him in Madison County. Percy had bought land there in 1811; in 1814 he settled on his property and began to develop a plantation. At the Walker's home he met Matilda's sister, Maria Pope, a great beauty, and in short order they were married.[21] Dr. Brown, on the other hand, came to Huntsville under far less happy circumstances. Early in 1813 Catherine Percy Brown had died following childbirth, and her bereaved husband brought his two children, Susan and James, to live on a plantation as near to his dear friend Walker as possible. By close companionship, Walker tried to ease the doctor's grief and to repay in some small measure the great debt he owed his friend.[22]

The marriage of Maria Pope to Tom Percy was a blow to James Sanders Walker. Eager to court Maria himself, he found it impossible because of the troublous times to leave his business and make the trip to Madison County. In the fall of 1811, cotton prices had fallen to an unprecedented low of eight cents a pound, and James Sanders' firm held large quantities of it. Through the War years of 1812-13, he could find no profitable market, but by 1814 he could at least report that in general the economic conditions of Georgia and South Carolina were improving. The wheat crop was large, and, with rice from the Low Country, would give "the preponderance in value to Bread Stuffs," he wrote. In spite of the state of cotton, he found the outlook encouraging enough to ask Walker if he would plead his cause with Maria.[23] He hoped to come to Huntsville that summer, he said. Then news reached him of the invasion of the Chesapeake area by the British. It was imperative that he go to Savannah, not only to protect his firm's cotton stored there, but to help in the defense of his country as a member of the first class militia. With great effort he supervised, in September and October, the movement of his company's cotton up the Savannah River to safety. He had the satisfaction of seeing some entrenchments laid out below the city and the stationing of some two or three thousand men for its defense. At least Savannah was guarded from a surprise attack, he felt. "A more respectable force" would be required to take the town "than will be probably sent by the enemy this winter." If the British chose to infest the Georgia coast, they could cut off the island trade via St. Mary's to Amelia, and Georgia would, in this event, do well even to hold Savannah, an opinion which was common enough to send the price of cotton down again.[24]

With the coming of peace, he saw a complete reversal of his fortunes. By February, 1815, cotton was bringing fourteen to sixteen cents a pound in Augusta, and by November the price was 25 cents. He and his partner held nearly 1,300 bales which were sold at a handsome profit. In December, funds of the firm in the Bank of Pennsylvania alone had risen to $54,296.60. Though in the meantime he had lost Maria to Tom Percy, he decided to move to the Alabama country anyway, and in 1816 he settled in Tuscaloosa, investing his fortune in town lots which yielded extremely profitable returns.[25] Once in Alabama, he served as one of his brother's political advisers.

War touched John Williams Walker, too, though perhaps more lightly. When General Andrew Jackson and General John Coffee came to the defense of the Territory against the Creeks in 1813 and 1814, they stopped with Walker en route to the Indian country. Coffee, a man James Sanders had described as "our relative," left a horse in Walker's care, but unfortunately the animal was killed by a falling tree, along with one of Walker's best plantation horses. In April, 1814, when Coffee was encamped at Hickory Ground in the Creek Nation, Walker wrote to tell him about the horse and to congratulate him "on the brilliant season, and glorious success of the army" in the campaign which culminated at Horseshoe Bend. A trace of the old hero-worship which Walker had once lavished on George Washington is evident in his letter about Jackson. Nothing "in all *our* Indian warfare equals or deserves to be compared with this Creek campaign," he declared. If the administration did not "make Jackson a Major General, I shall be astonished and beyond measure chagrined." The government deserved to be disgraced by incompetent commanders if it refused Jackson what he had "fairly earned," he told Coffee.[26]

Shortly thereafter Walker was instrumental in gaining for General Coffee a federal appointment to survey the Creek boundary lines, and an appointment for Coffee as surveyor of lands in the northern part of the Mississippi Territory followed in 1817. Coffee was an able and energetic surveyor, but he was also one of the most active trustees of the Cypress Land Company, the largest land speculator in the area. Colonel Pope, Thomas Bibb, and General Andrew Jackson were others who owned large blocks of Cypress Company stock and shared, unethically it would seem, in the profits derived from its favored position.[27]

Nonetheless it was probably Walker's solicitude for Coffee which prompted General Jackson to recommend Walker in June, 1817, for the governorship of the eastern half of the Territory should it be severed from Mississippi. Writing to President Monroe from Madison County, Jackson expressed "a firm belief that Major John W. Walker, a resident near Huntsville, is a man well qualified to fill that important office with honor to himself and profit to the country." There were "few who unite the necessary requisites, honesty and talents in a more eminent degree than Major Walker," the General wrote. The government should accede to the people's wish to have their governor chosen from among them since in this case "a man can be found who is well captivated [sic] for that office."[28]

Although this appointment was not forthcoming, 1817 was the year in which Walker began his rise to power. He had already identified himself with a number of causes the people seemed to favor—for example, a more liberal land policy. In 1814 he signed a petition objecting to a federal investigation of lands held under British claims. In the following year he joined others in pointing out to Congress the difficulties of those who had purchased land under the old credit system before the War of 1812. In order to obtain fertile swampland, many settlers had bought more land than they needed. Subsequently, loss of markets, Indian raids, and military service had combined to make it impossible for them to meet their payments. The petitioners asked that those who had bought more than one quarter-section be allowed to credit all their payments to one quarter section. Here was the essence of the relief law of 1821, for which Walker was to be largely responsible.[29] As flush times came, people remembered Walker as the man who knew the problems of land buying.

On the issue of the creation of the Alabama Territory and its subsequent admission to statehood Walker played a key role. He disagreed with the view, widely held in the Natchez area, which favored admitting the entire Mississippi Territory as one state. In 1812, the United States House of Representatives went so far as to pass a bill to this effect. Walker advised his good friend, Territorial Delegate George Poindexter, that he was against it because the area was too large. If erected it would have been larger than any state in the Union. *"And I love the Union too well to endanger it, even to render my own State powerful and pre-eminent,"* Walker wrote. He suggested that an east-west line dividing the Territory would remove the danger of jealousies between upcountry and low-country interests. Under his plan the Tombigbee and the Natchez settlements would have been admitted at once as the State of Mississippi, while the Alabama Territory would have included what later became northern Alabama and northern Mississippi. Poindexter, at first disposed to follow this advice, was disturbed by the annexation of West Florida parishes to the Territory, and came to favor a north-south dividing line. When William Lattimore succeeded Poindexter as territorial delegate in 1813, he at first opposed and then favored division. Interestingly enough, after the War of 1812, the Tombigbee and Natchez settlers reversed their positions on division. Seeing the great flow of settlers into the Alabama country, they sensed that the eastern section would one day come to dominate if one large state were erected, and the Natchez settlers began to favor division while the Tombigbee settlers opposed. Walker and the Madison County area consistently advocated division. In his efforts to achieve it, Walker made good use of important contacts with Georgia politicians.[30]

Charles Tait of Georgia, a United States Senator from 1809 to 1819, was chairman of the select committee dealing with the admission of Mississippi as a state. He was also one of Walker's intimate friends. Both men were from the Broad River area, where Tait "first bound" Walker with his regard. Tait was, in turn, equally intimate with Secretary of the Treasury William H. Crawford, one-time Senator and, from 1813 to 1815, Minister to France. Before he returned from Paris, Crawford had been appointed Secretary of War by Madison, and in October he was given the Treasury position, which he held throughout the

Monroe administration.[31] As Secretary of the Treasury he controlled enough patronage to more than maintain political contact with his followers in Georgia and those who had left Georgia to settle in the Mississippi Territory. Among the latter were W. W. Bibb, Bolling Hall, and Walker. These men with Tait and Crawford became leaders of the "Georgia Machine" in Alabama politics.

In January 1817, Walker replied to Tait's request for his opinion on the proper way to divide the Territory. He assured Tait that the eastern portion of the Mississippi Territory was not too large for a state, but by this time he had decided that an east-west line of division was unwise. "I love the Union more than any of its parts," he declared. He could not agree to such a division. He asked Tait to consider the Indian treaties of 1816, which would create an unbroken area for white settlements from the Tennessee to the Gulf. "Divide us, then, my dear Sir," he wrote, "by a N. and S. line, but be not too readily seduced by the idea of a natural boundary to establish the Tombigbee as the line." He reminded Tait that Georgia and South Carolina had experienced difficulties over the Savannah, and urged that the entire Tombigbee be given to Alabama so that disputes could be avoided.[32]

In spite of lusty objections from Dr. Lattimore, Mississippi's territorial delegate, and his allies, Tait obtained division of the Territory on substantially the lines Walker had outlined. Not only was the dividing line north-south, but a large part of the Tombigbee and the Port of Mobile were within the Alabama lines. Dr. Lattimore wrote Walker in March that Tait had played a strategic role, and Walker gratefully pledged Tait his support in any way possible.[33]

There followed, for Walker, a "new and unexpected

relation" to the people of Madison County. Because they knew of his part in the Territory's creation and approved it, he was immediately elected one of the County's representatives to the Territorial Legislature, scheduled to convene at St. Stephens in February 1818. Meanwhile, the "Georgians" in Washington began to parcel out the offices in the new Territory. To Dr. William Wyatt Bibb, former United States Representative and Senator, went the governorship. Bibb had been defeated in his campaign for re-election to the Senate, ostensibly because he had voted to increase congressional salaries. Appointed Governor, he resigned his Senate seat before his term had expired and looked forward with anticipation to joining former Broad River neighbors in Alabama, where he already owned land.[34]

Without conferring with Walker, Tait and Crawford drafted him as Secretary of the new Territory. "John Walker of Madison would willingly accept the office of Secretary," Crawford wrote the President-elect, "especially if Dr. Bibb should be appointed Governor—He is a man of fine talents, and strongly attached to the DR."[35] On December 16, 1817, Walker's appointment was issued. Secretary of State John Quincy Adams forwarded it to him at Lincolnton, North Carolina, the post town which he believed was nearest to Walker.[36]

Walker, however, did not accept. His health was poor and his family was growing. LeRoy Pope had been born on February 7, 1817, joining two other sons, John James and five-year-old Percy, named in honor of Tom Percy. St. Stephens, unconnected as it was by water routes with North Alabama, seemed too remote from Huntsville for the semi-permanent residence of a man with a sizable family. Furthermore, Walker's acceptance of the secretaryship would weaken Madison County's representation in the Territorial Legislature, and Madison County was already short of its proportional share of representatives in the territorial house.[37] But, though his decision was made, Walker could scarcely refuse his appointment until he had his commission in hand. On the last day of the congressional session, President Monroe, with no word from Walker and prompted by Bibb who desperately needed help, reluctantly nominated Henry Hitchcock to the post. It was not until the middle of May, almost a month after Hitchcock's confirmation, that Walker finally received his commission. He expressed his regret to the Secretary of State for the "tardy arrival" of the certificate, and voiced the hope that the situation "had not excited in the mind of the President any unpleasant feeling respecting the nomination of a Successor."[38] While this fiasco was drawing to a close, Walker had embarked on his active career as a territorial representative. In 1818, at 35, he had good cause to look with considerable satisfaction upon his achievements in the "new country." In eight years he had risen from obscurity and political defeat to a position of some importance. Furthermore, his popularity in Madison County seemed to promise him opportunities for greater public service in the future.

SIX

Alabama Politician

No LAWMAKER PLAYED A MORE PROMINENT ROLE IN THE first session of the Alabama Territorial Legislature than did John Williams Walker. Of the ten members present in St. Stephens at the opening session on January 19, 1818, four were from Madison County: Gabriel Moore, Hugh McVay, Clement C. Clay, and Walker. At the Legislative Council (Senate) on that first day, only one man was present, and that chamber transacted its affairs with unusual dispatch,[1] but the House got right to work. From the opening gavel, Walker was influential in procedural matters, and when committee assignments were made on the fourth day of the session he was placed on the powerful Ways and Means Committee, the Committee on Enrolled Bills, and a committee to superintend legislative printing and to examine the proof sheet of the House's standing rules.[2]

The first bill he introduced, dealing with banking in the Territory, initiated what would become a major issue in early Alabama politics and did much to label him as a conservative and a leader of the so-called "Royal Party," another name for the Georgia Machine. His bill was an amendment to the Mississippi Territory's Act of 1816 establishing the Planters and Mechanics Bank of Huntsville. Under it, the bank's name was to become the Planters and Merchants Bank of Huntsville, but more significantly, by it, the Alabama Territory would confirm the privileges granted under the earlier charter and would become eligible to purchase two-thirds of the bank's stock.

Walker was one of nine men to whom the original bank charter had been issued. The bank had opened for business, despite great opposition, in March 1817, with Colonel LeRoy Pope as its president and chief policy-maker. Governor Bibb opposed the amendment, and when the measure passed by a seven to four House vote, he cast the first veto in Alabama legislative history. In an able veto message the Governor maintained that the measure would commit the Territory to accept the bank's notes at face value for all obligations due it. He felt that the "very limited control" the Territory had over the bank would make such commitment unwise. He also strongly questioned the wisdom of allowing the bank to establish branches throughout the Territory. "According to my view of the subject," he told the House, "the powerful influence which is thus given to the Directors at Huntsville over the concern of the places where offices may be established, is worthy of consideration." While Huntsville was a flourishing town, center of an area boasting the largest population in the Territory, the Governor noted it was several hundred miles from "any sea port, and is not likely to become the principal seat of commerce." He held that it should have no peculiar claims to "the distribution and direction of banking establishments throughout the territory."[3]

Potent though the Governor's arguments were, Walker's committee, which received both message and vetoed bill, reported a similar bill to the House floor where it was quickly passed over Bibb's veto.[4]

Adding to Walker's reputation as a Royalist was the part he played in securing amendment of the Mississippi Territorial Act Against Usury. The measure, limiting the interest rate that could be charged for loans, made the borrowing of money next to impossible in the boom times of 1817-1818. Perhaps for this reason, a Washington County representative introduced an amendment providing that individuals might charge any interest rate so long as the rate was expressed in writing, but limiting the interest on bank loans and discounts to a maximum of six per cent and on personal loans to eight per cent when no amount of interest was prescribed in the note.[5] Walker aided in getting this measure approved by the Ways and Means Committee and passed by the House and Council to become law—a law which even from the most charitable viewpoint greatly favored the creditor class. With the coming of the 1819 panic, the amendment of the Usury Law became so unpopular that the first Legislature of the new State of Alabama had to repeal it. A considerable stigma accrued to Alabama's Georgia politicians for their roles in this episode, but Walker was so highly regarded as an individual and his services in other areas were judged so valuable that little opprobrium clung to him.

A number of other Walker proposals with far-reaching results show him to better advantage than his initial attempts. He introduced and led in the passage of a measure to remove the limitation on the territorial militia, which up to this time had been set at one brigade. Under this act, the Governor was authorized to call the militia at his discretion, and $2,000 was appropriated for support of "the people's army," from which sum the quartermasters could furnish their men with supplies. Walker gained popular favor with this democratic bill,[6] as he did with

steps taken to initiate internal improvements. Governor
Bibb's message to the Legislature had dealt at some length
with this question, and Walker served on and reported for
the committee which studied the Governor's suggestions.
As a result of his reports, the Legislature appointed a
commission, appropriating $3.00 per day for its pay, to
locate "the most suitable route for a road from the falls of
the Tuscaloosa, to the Tennessee River." It also memorialized the United States Congress to aid in the improvement of the navigation of the Tennessee.[7]

In addition, Walker fathered measures which enabled
Madison County to levy a special tax to complete her
public building; another authorizing the Governor to
draw upon the State of Mississippi for any monies due the
Alabama Territory; and still another which authorized the
taking of a territorial census.[8] When the session ended in
mid-February 1818, no representative had produced more
bills which were subsequently enacted than had Walker.
His orientation in territorial political life had been
thorough.

Madison County was pleased with Walker and showed
it. He was sent to the second, and final, session of the
Territorial Legislature in November, 1818, along with
Clement C. Clay and Samuel Walker. In the absence of
Gabriel Moore, Walker was elected Speaker of the House.
"This Station relieves me from the labor of composition
and the drudgery committee business," he wrote. Despite
the laborious work of dealing with a group of twenty men
most of whom were new members unfamiliar with parliamentary procedure, he now had more time to devote to his
major interest—securing statehood for Alabama.[9] In this
mission, he naturally turned to his good friend, Senator
Charles Tait, for aid.

Tait, a lame-duck in 1818 (like Bibb he had voted to increase congressional salaries and his political opponents made the most of it), had thought of resigning and going to Alabama at once, as Bibb had done. Walker urged him not to do this. "I regard you as the Patron of Alabama," he wrote, "and would feel your absence as a sinister move." When Walker learned that the Senator had sold his Georgia plantation and was making preparations to move, he wrote him, "No man rejoices more than I do that you have selected Alabama for your residence." But Walker urged that in his last hours in the Senate, he make Alabama dearer to himself by making himself dearer to Alabama. "I think you ought to crown your other labors of love and kinship by procuring the act of her admission into the Union," he declared. His labors would make admission in the winter of 1818-1819 "doubly sure" and bring Alabama in under the most advantageous terms.[10]

Under a policy initiated in 1787 and followed thereafter, a Territory could demand admission when it had 60,000 free inhabitants; yet, Walker reminded Tait, in no case with which he was acquainted had Congress waited until a Territory demanded admission. It seemed to be mandatory only that a Territory have a population of 35,000, the number required for electing one member to the House of Representatives. When Mississippi was admitted in 1817 she had had 47,000 inhabitants. A census of Alabama taken in the fall of 1818 had indicated the Territory could count 67,594 inhabitants, 21,000 of them slaves, exclusive of Marion and Lawrence Counties whose returns were not in. Thus, Walker said, he believed that Alabama was "more populous than any other territory at the time of its admission," and he felt confident that she would have more than 60,000 free inhabitants when Congress next met. In

his opinion, three-fifths of the slaves should be counted in
computing population for the Territory's admission because slavery was legal in Alabama. If slaves could be
counted in determining House representation, they should
also be counted to meet admission requirements.

Furthermore, Tait was informed, the enabling act authorizing Alabama to hold a constitutional convention
must assure proper apportionment of representation. Tait
would not have "thoroughly played" his part until he saw
this done. Walker obviously feared Madison County,
the most populous in the Territory, might be under-
represented. It was not that he sought special consideration
for North Alabama, but the "intrigue and low cunning
and logrolling" plaguing the Territorial Legislature could
result in grossly unfair apportionment. He hoped the
Legislature would leave apportionment to the Congress,
but if it refused to do so he promised to inform Tait where
a correction could be made.[11]

Walker's fears proved justified when efforts were made
to limit some counties' representation, yet in the end the
Legislature designed a fair apportionment. Nevertheless,
the basic sectionalism which has characterized Alabama
history, often in the antebellum period cutting across party
lines, asserted itself. The measure was "saddled with a
ryder" giving legal recognition to a fait accompli of
Governor Bibb. Brought in by the South Alabama men,
the rider provided that Cahaba, a settlement at the confluence of the Cahaba and Alabama Rivers, should be the
permanent seat of territorial government.

The question of a location for the seat of government
had been argued for some time. The first session of the
Territorial Legislature had appointed a commission to
make recommendations. While the members deliberated,

Governor Bibb used his contacts with the Georgians in Washington to obtain passage of an act granting the Alabama Territory a section of land "to be located under the direction of the Governor of the said Territory, for the seat of government therein." In the summer of 1818 while visiting in Georgia, Bibb read that the law had been passed, and from the same journal he learned that by presidential proclamation the lands of the Cahaba area were to be offered for sale in October, 1818. Returning to the Territory, he examined the Cahaba lands, confirmed his belief that here was the ideal site, and exercised his prerogative under the law to choose it for the capital. Somewhat later the legislative commission, headed by C. C. Clay, reported in favor of Tuscaloosa.

Governor Bibb wrote Tait that his action had "given much displeasure to the Madison folk and the people on the Warrior." He advised him to see that the President did not yield on the matter, for if he did, there would be "some collision" in the next legislative session in Alabama. "What I believed right I have done," the Governor declared, "and with the help of the Lord I shall pursue the same course hereafter; whatever may be the consequence." Almost as an afterthought he added that it was impossible to make a selection that would please all areas.[12] Now, he used the influence of his office, the South Alabama political strength, and the assistance of his Georgia friends to gain approval of the rider.

Walker revered Bibb, and he and his followers did not join in the clamor of objections raised by other North Alabamians. "We acquiesced in the opinion of the majority . . . altho' we deprecate the mode in which the thing was done," Walker wrote, in what was for him strong criticism of the Governor. He observed that he and the

northern representatives could have influenced the Council
to kill the rider, but since four representatives from North
Alabama were absent this would have created an impasse.
Thus an *"accidental* majority" was allowed to have its
way.[13]

After the fall session of the Legislature, the Governor
sought to rationalize his position in a letter to Secretary
Crawford. He asked for authority to select any 640 acres at
Cahaba to save himself from serious embarrassment and
then reviewed the dispute. "Owing to the accidental
circumstances of the northern part of the territory having
been first settled and therefore at the present time being
the most populous," he reported, the movement to fix the
seat of government at the "falls of the Warrior" was almost
irresistible. Basing his decision, he said, on a longer, more
mature view, he had selected a *"Permanent seat* of government," feeling that a census taken in two years, or even
one, would validate his choice.[14]

With Crawford's aid Bibb was given a free hand and
won a temporary victory. Yet the question was still of some
concern in the Constitutional Convention in 1819, and it
remained a bitter point with Walker who, as a political
friend of Bibb, had to defend Bibb's act to his own
constituents in North Alabama.

The apportionment bill itself, on the other hand,
aroused no controversy. Walker, transmitting it to Tait to
have it incorporated in the enabling act, wrote, "I should
think the *number* fixed by this act sufficient," but if it must
be changed, it could only be justly done by doubling all the
counties' representation.[15] He asked Tait to set the time for
the election of delegates and for the Constitutional Convention, suggesting that they be not long delayed, but that
there be two months between them.

Meanwhile the Legislature authorized the sale of two lots in Cahaba and the use of $10,000 from the proceeds for the erection of temporary government buildings. With the Governor's approval, Huntsville was chosen the temporary seat of government, which Walker felt was "as it should be." "You will of course," he wrote Tait, "appoint it as the place at which the Convention will assemble." He urged Tait to try to obtain, as an additional boon to Alabama, two Representatives for the state upon its admission. Since no other territory had been so populous as Alabama at the time of admission two representatives seemed to him equitable.[16]

The second session of the Territorial Legislature came to an end after two fatiguing, eleven-hour days. Walker started home the next day, November 20, covering about 250 miles in six days and 58 miles the last day. Once home at Oakland be wrote Senator Tait again, urging him to continue his fight for statehood. If "you can only give us two Representatives in Congress at the first, you shall be immortalized by the good people of Alabama," he said. Though he himself may have played "the great man at St. Stephens," Walker knew his success depended on Tait's achievements as an "effective Delegate of the Territory." He was confident that his predictions about Tait's accomplishments would not cause him to be known hereafter as a false prophet.[17]

When Tait's enabling act reached Alabama, in January 1819, all the Georgians were pleased. Governor Bibb felt that only two improvements were possible: the removal of minimum residence requirements for voters who would elect delegates to the Constitutional Convention, and placing the sale of school land at the discretion of the State Legislature.[18] Walker was delighted that "something more" had been written into the act than the usual provisions on a state's behalf. The act reserved two sections of land for the endowment of a university, so that an institution of higher learning could be opened "on the most liberal and satisfactory foundation." Further, over the protests of Mississippi, the western boundary of Alabama was left intact, giving the new state most of the Tombigbee River. "Your view of the subject is undoubtedly correct," Walker wrote Tait. "It would be monstrous to annex us to Mississippi against *our consent.*"

Tait had been unable to obtain more than one Representative for the state in spite of Walker's belief that the Territory had 75,000 people in early 1819. But internally, the enabling act's apportionment was simple justice in Walker's opinion. Some might protest that the Tennessee Valley would have too large a voice in the Convention, but the apportionment accorded with the population. "If God and nature have bestowed on us a fertile soil and a happy climate, and put it into the hearts of multitudes to desire to cast their lot among us, are we to blame for it?" Walker asked. Above all, a Constitutional Convention, "which is emphatically the act of the People themselves," should have full and equal representation. Walker thought it regrettable that all the people in the Territory could not assemble for this work. He was sorry that Tait could not be a member of the Convention, but he urged him to "make me the depository of your plans and opinions—at least as far as you can make me a convert to them. In the great outlines I think we should agree without much dispute."[19]

Walker would have been pleased to devote his full time to his family and plantation, but instead he announced his candidacy in April as a Madison County delegate to the Constitutional Convention. Though he recoiled in "utter repugnance" from all the vulgarity of electioneering" and vowed to leave the people "to decide for themselves without solicitation or tricks," he hoped to "render the state some service." If he were successful in the Convention, he knew his friends would insist that he "accept some office of considerable trust in the state," and it was generally agreed that he could easily be elected to the United States House of Representatives. In fact, a "vast majority of the last legislature" had offered him a Senate seat. But Walker believed if Bibb chose to continue in public life the Senate would be his preference and he felt that the Governor should have his choice of positions. "I would be the last man to oppose him," Walker proclaimed. Personally, he would not care for the office of Governor of Alabama, being "tied down to the irksome routine of office, without the means of improvement from books and superior men" which might be enjoyed in Washington. Of all the offices in the gift of a state, the Senate seat was the one Walker preferred, "not only for its dignity," but for the contacts and manner of life it afforded. "Hoping to substitute zeal and integrity for talents," if it were offered him, he would accept it, he avowed, his health permitting. By February, 1819, Walker had gone thirty months without breaking a blood vessel, but even so some of his friends were apprehensive about a Senate seat for him. With more concern than tact one of them reminded him that it would be better to be a "living Governor than a dead Senator." He decided to postpone his decision until after the Constitutional Convention.[20] And in the interim, President Monroe on March 2, 1819, with Senate approval, appointed Walker United States Territorial Judge. Senator Tait had nominated Oliver H. Prince of Georgia, and John Pope had endorsed John P. Oldham for the position.[21] "The appointment was asked without my knowledge," Walker wrote, "and in the teeth of my known wishes; but I have been compelled, by a sense of public duty, to accept it for the short period which remains of our Territorial career." He resigned in September, after the adoption of the Alabama Constitution.

Madison countians cast 2,323 votes in the election for delegates to the Constitutional Convention. Running in a field of 22, Walker was fifth among the eight successful candidates, the third place winner exceeding him by only ten votes, and the fourth place, by just one. The ballot listed another "John Walker" as a candidate by unfortunate happenstance, and all undifferentiated Walker votes were split between them. "I did succeed," Walker wrote, "notwithstanding the usury law, the judgeship, and my laziness, and my obstinate adherence to my unfashionable non-electioneering course, and a thousand *et ceteras*." He felt he could have been first had he desired first place enough to wage a fighting campaign. As it was, it was generally held that he had "a better *right* to be pleased than any other candidate." "I do not care a whiff of this," he wrote. "I am elected, and on my own terms—and that is enough."[22]

In the interval before the convention opened, Walker worked at developing his ideas on the features which should be included in the new Constitution. "I am cobbling up a Constitution for Alabama," he wrote Tait, "such a one as I deem the best for her." Walker believed that in ascribing great power to him Tait was overestimating his influence in the coming session, but Walker vowed that what influence he had would be exerted "for *honest* purposes." Contrary to Tait's expectation, Walker anticipated grave differences of principle among the delegates, with the question of representation causing the most trouble. "I am no party man," Walker wrote, "and I will not be one. I look at the whole, and not simply at a part. . . . I will be moderate and cool myself and will attempt to infuse into the whole body the spirit of conciliation . . . and moderation."[23]

In late April Senator Tait came to Huntsville, one of two distinguished guests to appear that spring, and Walker presided at a dinner in his honor April 21. Among the toasts was one to the convention, praying that it "would be guided by an enlightened and disinterested patriotism, and terminate in a Constitution which shall secure to our latest posterity the blessings of liberty." Tait addressed the dinner and closed with a toast to Alabama which prayed that "the wisdom of her Councils [may] equal those advantages which nature has bestowed upon her."[24]

Scarcely a month later President Monroe, accompanied only by his secretary and an army lieutenant, arrived in a surprised Huntsville and put up at the Inn. A citizens' committee headed by C. C. Clay waited upon him at once and invited him to a public dinner the following day. This affair was presided over by Colonel Pope and attended by 100 Madison countains, but the next day the presidential party on its way to Nashville, "stopped two or three hours" at Walker's "cabin." "We sustained him a mid-day which [was] a sort of second breakfast," the host reported. "His extreme plainness, and the simplicity of his manners were matters of surprise to many. He was very affable, and of easy access to all: and—what may not be deemed altogether wonderful—and decidedly quite a popular man!"[25]

These diversions over, Huntsville awaited the opening of the Convention. On July 5, at the opening session, John Williams Walker was immediately and unanimously elected President of the Convention, sixteen of whose members were from South Alabama, 28 from the north. A delegate from the south recalled:

> It soon became manifest that it would not be an easy manner to agree on the principles and details of a Constitution [because the Convention] was composed of members from different states, and each one bringing with him all the partialities and prejudices of state preference. [To bring order into the negotiations] it was resolved by the convention [July 6] that a committee of fifteen should be appointed by the President, whose duties were to draft a skelliton [sic] constitution.[26]

This was agreed to after resolutions to establish both a 22-man and a 20-man committee had been defeated.[27]

Walker apparently had a free hand in selecting the committee, and he chose as its chairman his good friend Clement C. Clay. Walker's most important work in the convention may well have been done at this point, for it would seem only logical for him to turn over to Clay the rough draft of the Constitution upon which he had been working. Since the committee's draft received few modifications from the floor, it is not entirely unreasonable to assume that Walker framed much of the final Constitution.

On July 7, the Convention adopted rules for its conduct, granting the President, surprisingly enough for the times, a great deal of power, including the right to speak and vote on all questions and authority to preserve order and compel members to attend.[28] On July 13, Clay read the committee's draft of the Constitution to the Convention—a draft which it is generally conceded envisaged a moderately liberal government,[29] but not such a radically democratic government as the Jacksonians would bring to the West a few years later. Walker's influential role in the Convention was sustained throughout the debates which followed the committee's presentation. As he had anticipated, representation proved to be the most bitterly divisive issue. The original provision held that a voter must be "a white man and a member of the militia (unless exempt by law from military service) , that the Federal ratio should be the basis of apportionment in the state legislature, [and] that annual elections and annual sessions of the legislature be provided."[30] In the ensuing discussion, Walker electrified the Committee of the Whole when he proposed that none "but free white persons" should be counted in determining representation in the Legislature. Many of the southern counties vigorously opposed deletion of the accepted federal "three-fifths clause" because they stood to gain representation by it, but Walker's amendment carried, and was considered a crucial change.

South Alabama leaders countered with the first of a series of attacks on the system of apportioning which would give consideration to population. Walker's friend Henry Hitchcock of Washington County proposed an amendment providing that no district should be entitled to more than one Senator. According to the *Alabama Republican* this proposal "produced a much more animated debate than any question which had previously been brought before the committee, in which gentlemen of the first talents in the Convention participated." Walker, C. C. Clay, and other Madison County delegates opposed the amendment, as might be expected, while Hitchcock, Judge Harry Toulmin of Baldwin County, William R. King of Dallas County, and Israel Pickens of Washington County supported it. When, on the second day of the debate, Hitchcock saw that the measure would never carry, he proposed

a face-saving amendment which was passed without discussion. This divided the state into senatorial districts
based on population, each of which was entitled to elect
one Senator. The Senate's membership was restricted to no
less than one-fourth nor more than one-third of the House.
The *Alabama Republican* adjudged that a major issue had
been settled on the bases of "equity and justice." But the
dispute over representation was far from settled. Near the
end of the Convention John D. Bibb of Montgomery
County proposed to remove a clause which gave a separate
Representative to any town having a number of residents
equal to the ratio fixed for a Representative. Walker
joined 24 of his colleagues to defeat the measure, but the
opposition countered with a shrewd maneuver: To delete
the section on senatorial representation and substitute a
provision giving one Senator to each county except Madison, which would have two. This measure was defeated
when Walker, as President, cast the deciding negative
ballot to break a tie vote.[31] Judge Toulmin then offered an
amendment which would increase proportionately the
population required for each Representative beyond the
first two each county was entitled to elect. Walker assisted
in defeating this by a vote of 23 to 19, but surprisingly
enough Clay and some other North Alabama delegates
voted for the amendment.

Toulmin's final effort was an amendment providing that
no county should be entitled to more than five representatives. After its defeat by a vote of 22 to 20, the basic
agreement on representation remained intact.[32] The archi-
tects of Alabama's first Constitution could be confident
that the political power of larger counties would accord
with their population, and an important principle of
democratic government had been sustained.

Walker used his influence to promote progressive policies on two other issues. He helped defend a clause, in
keeping with the frontier spirit which still prevailed in
Alabama, limiting the Legislature's appointments in the
state militia to adjutant general and quartermaster general.
The defense proved successful, whereupon he joined with
a minority which was unsuccessful in removing all legislative power to make appointments in the militia, leaving
selections to popular election by the men.[33] Although he
had voted against the provision for popular election of
court clerks, once the measure had passed, he opposed
attempts to tamper with it by requiring fitness tests for the
positions. C. C. Clay proposed that the supreme or circuit
courts certify the fitness of clerks, and when this proposal
was defeated, Judge Toulmin countered with a plan to
require clerks to stand an examination within six months
of their election and to vacate their offices following the
next election if found to be incompetent.[34] Walker joined
the majority to defeat this amendment.

On the question of the judiciary Walker was a thorough
conservative. According to the original draft, judges were
to be appointed by the Legislature and were to hold office
during good behavior. This measure was attacked by
revisionists who sought to limit judges to a six-year term,
but were defeated in the attempt 18 to 25, Walker voting
with the majority. A decade later general disgust with
judicial decisions resulted in the demand for popular
election of judges, and a measure to provide for it became
the Constitution's first amendment.[35]

The proposed Constitution had authorized the establishment of a state bank by a two-thirds legislative vote, and
permitted the Legislature to establish one new branch in
each session. But no bank could be established unless the

Legislature subscribed two-fifths of its stock and appointed directors equal to the state's interest. Further, no bank was to go into operation until the payment in bullion of the amount of the stock subscribed, not less than $100,000. Each stockholder was made liable for the debts of the bank to the amount of his stock.[36] In late July the Convention considered a proposal to reduce from two-thirds to one-half the legislative vote required to establish a state bank. Walker supported the measure but saw it go down to defeat. Though he had maintained an attitude of friendly encouragement toward banks, this vote scarcely branded him the tool of special interests, for no effort was made to change the other requirements in the banking clause.

The question of the state capital arose to haunt Governor Bibb once more. Tuscaloosa's Marmaduke Williams endeavored to modify the Constitution's requirement that all sessions of the Legislature after the first be held at Cahaba, at least until 1825. Williams' amendment would have empowered the first session of the Legislature to choose a capital site. Walker, hoping not to reopen an old wound, joined the majority in a 25 to 6 vote to defeat the measure, much to Governor Bibb's pleasure. Bibb obviously believed that by 1825 Cahaba would be so flourishing a town that no one would think of moving the capital. He continued to be confident that the southern portion of the state would outstrip the north and vindicate his high-handed action of the previous year.[37]

The 44 delegates to the Constitutional Convention signed the new Constitution of Alabama on August 2, 1819. The signing completed, Israel Pickens offered the following unanimously adopted resolution: "*Resolved, that the thanks of this Convention be presented to John W. Walker, President, thereof, for the dignity, ability and*

impartiality with which he has discharged the arduous
duties of the Chair."

Walker's reply stressed the harmony which had in general characterized the Convention.

> . . . while I have life, I shall never cease to cherish a
> grateful recollection of the uniform kindness and sup-
> port of this enlightened Conventional. . . . Our labours
> are now at an end. We have given to the State of Alabama
> a Constitution—not indeed perfect—not precisely such
> as any one individual of this community, would, unas-
> sisted, have framed in his closet. [Yet it is] emphatically
> republican and such as gives us a clear and indisputable
> title, to admission into the great family of the Union.

He pointed out that by the process of amendment which it
provided, the Constitution could in the end be molded by
the people, and continued:

> It proclaims the great first principles of liberty [in that]
> it guards the equal rights of all. . . . the offspring of
> mutual concession and compromise, it occupies that mid-
> dle ground on which a majority was found to unite.[38]

Shortly after the close of the Convention, Walker wrote
Tait that it had "moved very harmoniously" and had
framed "a very good Constitution. . . . It is not exactly
such as I could wish, but on the whole there are few
better," he commented.[39]

Some years later John D. Bibb, who had from time to
time opposed Walker during the floor fight over representation, wrote that Walker "was considered to be decidedly the most talented member of the convention." At
the time, Bibb recalled, the Convention's president "was
much emaciated and his physical powers greatly weakened
by consumption," yet he "presided with dignity and im-

partiality and gave entire satisfaction to all parties." His "refined manners, . . . powers of elocution, . . . and statesman suavity . . . commanded the entire attention of the members of the convention whenever he attempted to address the body. . . . On several occasions he displayed great wisdom and talent in the speeches he made."[40]

The role he had played here probably insured Walker's election to the United States Senate. The Georgians in Huntsville took stock of Alabama's political picture and planned their strategy with care. Governor Bibb had no interest in a Senate seat, contrary to Walker's earlier assessment, and with Bibb out, Walker was free to accept. The Royalists would have attempted to secure the second senatorship for Charles Tait, but expediency dictated that this seat must go to South Alabama, while the machine filled the other major offices of the new state. To prepare the way, Walker resigned as a federal judge in September, using poor health as his excuse. When, in November, the first Alabama Assembly met, the South Alabamians chose Colonel William Rufus King as their candidate, and he and Walker were promptly elected to the Senate.

Governor Bibb seems to have pulled the strings on this maneuver, since both Tait and Crawford were disappointed. "Your short residence here, and the jealousy of Georgia influence which the idea of Governor and both Senators may create, make this caution proper," Bibb wrote Tait. Since the "murmurs of 'Georgia Faction' " had begun to be raised, Tait had no choice but to understand. He declared himself content, if it was not possible to present him as a candidate without "disturbing the harmony of our political leaders."[41] Knowing Tait was eager to remain in the Senate, Secretary Crawford had sought to buy King off with the Huntsville Land Office Receivership

"If he is not politically mad he will accept it," Crawford
wrote Tait, but he urged Tait to conceal his role in the
matter because its general knowledge might "be of *no use*
to you, but the contrary." King refused the bait, however,
and Tait applied to Walker and Crawford for the post of
Federal Judge for the Alabama District, a position also
sought by two others. William Crawford, a member of the
Georgians in Alabama, promptly withdrew when he
learned that Tait wanted the job, and received appointment instead as United States District Attorney. On the
other hand, Judge Harry Toulmin, who had served for
fourteen years as a judge in the Mississippi and Alabama
territories and was said to have one of the finest legal minds
in Alabama, was not affiliated with the faction and remained a candidate for judge until the end. He wrote
Walker asking his aid and styling himself his friend, much
to the Senator's amusement.

As soon as Walker arrived in Washington, he went
"directly to the palace" and "took the liberty in three
words" of telling the President he wanted the judgeship for
Tait. With Secretary Crawford and Calhoun aiding, the
appointment was quickly granted, and the Senate gave its
unanimous approval, even Tait's former opponents speaking of him in "good set terms of praise."[42]

While this dispute was in progress Bibb was elected the
first Governor of the State of Alabama. The Georgia
Machine, tallying the vote, was frightened. Bibb's majority
over the Tuscaloosa attorney, Marmaduke Williams, was
only 1,202 out of a total vote of 15,482. In Madison
County, where the Governor's selection of Cahaba for the
capital site still rankled, Bibb won by only five votes out of
2,453. Secretary Crawford presumed "the old leaven of
party in Georgia has been effervescing in Alabama. . . .

some of his quandam [sic] friends . . . have been hostile
to him and to his views."[43]

During the first session of the State Legislature, Walker,
far away in Washington, heard conflicting evaluations of
its work. Acting on Bibb's advice, the session authorized
the sale or lease of school lands and allowed counties to
allot portions of their funds for improvement of streams. It
created six new counties, and passed many measures of a
police and housekeeping nature. Reviewing its accomplishments, the newly arrived Georgia politician John Mc-
Kinley wrote Walker, "Certainly you had a *wise well
informed and honest* Legislature let *envy* and *malice* say
what they may." But J. W. Taylor, another prominent
Madison countian, held another view. "I hope, my dear
Walker," he wrote, "that you have found a much wiser
legislative body at Washington, than the one you left in
session in Huntsville." He believed the first Legislature
would become a byword unless all of its laws were repealed
within a year or so. He questioned the wisdom of many of
the laws enacted and held that the lawmakers acted un-
constitutionally in electing a quartermaster general and an
adjutant general without first authorizing such action by
passing a law.[44]

The reign of the Royal Party was rapidly drawing to a
close. Early in 1820 Governor Bibb was thrown from a
horse, sustaining serious injuries which, with subsequent
complications, caused his death in the summer.[45] While he
lay ill and confined to his room through the long spring,
Judge Tait appraised the situation for Walker.

> [In case of Bibb's death] the affairs of our new state
> [will] be again exposed to great agitation and peril. [If
> he] could be spared a few years, his official station, his
> talents and his conciliatory manners would greatly tend

to settle the State in a proper course of policy—to silent
the pretensions of little men and promote our general
prosperity.[46]

Tait was sure that he had detected a change in attitude
toward Bibb since his election. "I think the time is not
distant when you and your friends will see that no good
man in the state shall be opposed to you," he told the
Governor.[47] But the Governor did not live to prove Tait
right, and upon his death was succeeded by his far less
astute brother Thomas, who had been president of the
State Senate.

Attorney General Hitchcock, Walker's good friend, kept
the Senator informed on the actions of the Legislature in
the 1820 session—a session disastrous for the Georgia Party.
Local bills consumed most of the time, many of them
calculated "more to secure the popularity of the individuals who introduced them" than for any good they would
do. "The Governor makes a great talk about *internal*
improvements," Hitchcock wrote, as the politicians set up
an advisory board. "With much difficulty a character for a
State Bank was passed which, "the Attorney General felt,
"if it can be carried into effect will be a safe institution."
The bank was to be capitalized at $2,000,000, the sum to be
raised through popular subscription, because Georgia leaders preferred it to subscription by the state government.
Unfortunately the money could not be raised, and the state
bank issue remained troublesome. Only "five laws of a
general nature" were passed during the entire session,
among them acts creating three new counties, and a
measure authorizing former Judge Toulmin to prepare a
digest of the state's laws.[48] Among the laws not passed was a
reapportionment measure, a clear violation of the Constitution.[49] Hitchcock felt that Thomas Bibb's inept leadership

had much to do with the session's failure. "His want of decision and some worse traits of character are showing themselves in many acts and to some in such a degree as to create disgust in some who heretofore have thought better of him." The absence of a "man of commanding influence" resulted in "sectional jealousies springing up on every question," Hitchcock said.[50]

Opposition to the Georgia faction came to focus in the manipulations of Washington County's Israel Pickens, a former North Carolinian, who announced for Governor in 1821.[51] Pickens wrote Walker that he had sacrificed "something of feeling as well as interest" in making the race. His one-time friendship with the Georgians made him avow a "predilection for peace," but he "could not . . . well avoid the course" he had taken.[52] Sensing the need to mend political fences at home, Walker wrote Hitchcock immediately, offering to serve as the faction's candidate for Governor in 1821, but the Georgians had chosen Dr. Henry Chambers of Madison County to make the race, convinced, Hitchcock told Walker, that "we have at least acted safely and perhaps saved you from the mortification of a defeat, and considering the unpleasant result of the deliberations of the legislature in adjourning without making an apportionment, I think you may well congratulate yourself on being released from the trouble of the contest."[53] Walker's role in 1818 in the passage of the Usury Law, and his close connection with the Planters and Merchants Bank of Huntsville were without doubt the real reasons he was rejected. Pickens could be counted upon to attack both of these vulnerable points with every weapon at hand. The courts were still litigating cases stemming from the Usury Law, now repealed, and the Bank had been forced by the panic of 1819-20 to suspend its specie payments, although the Legislature still allowed its notes to be received at par in payment of state obligations.

After a campaign in which he appealed to the voters on the questions of currency, a state bank, and the domination of "Georgia" men, Pickens was overwhelmingly elected. Hitchcock lamented that Chambers had carried only a small part of northern Alabama. "What course Mr. Pickens will take I do not know," he wrote, but "his capacity for low intrigue will probably enable him to keep the popular vain [sic] on his side."[54] Walker, whose career is alone a vindication of Georgian leadership, was to remain in Washington until 1822. Although there is a possibility he could have been elected Governor, there can be no doubt that he served Alabama to greatest advantage in the Senate where he won acclaim not only for himself but for his state as well.

SEVEN

Missouri, Slavery, and Power Politics

In late November, 1819, Walker left Huntsville for Washington. The weeks before his departure had been chaotic, his home filled with friends and well-wishers, guests and office seekers from morning to night. In part they came to express their amazement at the rapidity with which Walker had been transformed from frontier planter to United States Senator. Larkin Newby, his boyhood friend, expressed the general surprise in a note. "In the last six months I have scarcely been able to keep in sight of you . . . for altho your course has not been excentric, yet it has been . . . rapid. [First I heard] 'J. W. W. one of the Judges of our Supreme Court is appointed President (of the Convention)'—next that 'J. W. W., President of our late Convention, has been appointed one of our Senators to Congress.' "[1]

Because Tom Percy was delegated to take charge of Oakland, Walker was sure the plantation would cause him little concern in his absence. His health was, as always, a nagging worry, but the greatest wrench was taking leave of his family, and the arrival in late October of another child made the parting doubly hard. The baby, named Charles in honor of Charles Tait, was "easily the finest of the four" sons, in his father's opinion.[2] Tait, ruminating over Walker's new opportunity to "do good on a large scale," wrote that he hoped Walker would be more successful than he had been. For himself, he said, he found the best intentions to be misinterpreted, and he had obtained solace only by keeping faith with himself.[3] The fact that Walker's first days in Washington were occupied in securing political appointment for Tait is indicative of the close attachment of the two men.

Walker arrived in the capital the first week in December and spent some time inspecting the new halls of Congress, which he thought "very splendid and magnificent." He later came to modify this first impression, finding them "better adapted to show than use." Their acoustics proved so bad that debate within their walls was a hardship on both speaker and listener. On December 7, 1819, Alabama's first Senator produced his credentials, "was qualified and took his seat in the Senate." It was not until the following day that the resolution for the admission of the state into the Union passed both chambers and was sent to the President. On December 22, upon Senate approval of a motion made by Senator Thomas H. Williams of Mississippi, Walker and William Rufus King drew lots to determine when their terms would expire. By hazard it was decided that Walker's would be the six-year term and King's the four.[4]

The two new senators were plummeted headlong into the middle of the struggle over statehood for Missouri, now in its second year of vociferous debate. "Of all the important questions which presented themselves to the consideration of Congress," Walker wrote, "that of Missouri is the most threatening and dangerous."[5] As Senator Nathaniel

Macon of North Carolina expressed it, the "want of money by the Government and by the people at home, as well as the contest between the U.S.B. [United States Bank] and the state banks, together with the dispute with Spain; seem to be entirely forgotten in this question. . . ."[6] Walker called it "the most obvious and fearful of all possible descriptions of party questions," since it was "defined and circumscribed by sectional or geographical lines." It arrayed one part of the Union against another. "It is believed by some and feared by others," he declared, "that it is merely the entering wedge—and that it posits directly to a total emancipation of the blacks."[7] It was most unfortunate that the question had not been settled in the previous congressional session. On the other hand, he was confident that the Senate would stand by its former decision to admit Missouri without restrictions on slavery, so there was no cause for despair.[8]

From St. Stephens, Israel Pickens echoed Walker's fears. In his opinion the slavery question as connected with the admission of Missouri presented the most "serious difficulties" at that time and would do so in future years.[9] Tait, writing now from Alabama, viewed the question as the "most delicate and most difficult of all." During the previous session, he had served as chairman of the Senate committee concerned with the problem, and on at least two occasions had spoken at length on the subject. But he seemed to take pride in the fact that, unlike Rufus King of New York, he had not made his address "a text" and had not written essays on the question for the general public. He pledged himself never to "cater for popular notice in that way."[10]

It is obvious from his letters that to Tait the villain of the piece was New York's King. A dangerous man, he warned Walker; one against whom Walker should be on guard if King were re-elected in 1820. "Plausible, cunning, insidious and insincere," Tait called him. True, he possessed a great knowledge of public affairs; true, he had valuable experience. But he was, when all was said and done, a "New York politician—the end sanctifies the means." Tait looked for him to exploit the Missouri question to the hilt. If the Senate could be made to stand by its previous decision to let Missouri treat slavery as it saw fit, all would be well; this was all the South wanted—at the time. But, "it is political power that the northern folk are in pursuit of," he wrote. If the non-slaveholding states could be induced "to make a stand against them which tolerate slavery and should become the majority," he warned, "the management of the Genl. Govt. will pass into their hands with all its power and patronage." To "attain this [was] the *sole* view of the *knowing ones*," said Judge Tait.[11]

There can be no doubt that Tait's suspicions of King were shared by many another Southerner. A strong Federalist, King had been the party candidate for Vice-President in 1804 and again in 1808, and had been selected to run for President in 1816 against James Monroe. He was not a disunionist, but he appeared to Southern observers to have a marked phobia of the South. He "was interested in securing predominance for his section within the Union."[12] Yet when Tait expressed his views on King to his good friend John C. Calhoun, Calhoun was quick to disagree. He was aware that many "virtuous and well informed citizens to the South [felt that] a premeditated struggle for superiority" had begun between the North and the South, but he did not think so. No doubt some Northerners would like for private reasons to see such a struggle, since a majority of the votes in Congress and the electoral college came from non-slaveholding states. He believed the number of these Northerners to be very small, however, and "to be found almost wholly in New York, and the middle states." In his opinion the restrictionists were "actuated by a variety of motives," the vast majority of which were "perfectly honest. Very few indeed look to emancipation."[13]

In spite of Calhoun's opinions, Tait believed his own diagnosis was correct and so informed Walker.[14] He advocated discussion of the Missouri issue in Southern state legislatures, and believed the South should make it a common cause because a question greater than that of power rested therein. It was, the Judge felt, a problem of personal liberty. At the same time he expressed the hope that the Congress would be wise enough to make two states of the Missouri Territory granting greater political strength to the slave states. If he could aid in securing this one advantage, Tait said, he would feel that he had not lived in vain.[15]

The attempt to nurture Walker's concern was hardly necessary. It grew apace. Agitation of the question was "menacing us with alarming evils. . . . The iniquity of slavery in the abstract, and even the slave trade itself, are confounded with: a question purely constitutional," he wrote.[16] In the winter of 1819-1820, essays and pamphlets streamed from the northern presses, and northern cities called daily public meetings to harangue on the subject. Walker looked with dismay upon this dispute which was "becoming a mere contest for power,—the *free* states striving to seize the control of the Union under the mask of affected humanity."[17] This opinion was shared by many Southerners, among them Alabama's Attorney General,

Henry Hitchcock, who wrote that "political sectional power" was at issue. When he viewed the entire situation, he was extremely doubtful as to the destiny of the Union.[18]

The moral principle injected in the Missouri controversy was incomprehensible—even absurd—to Walker. From his boyhood he had owned slaves; the property left him by his father's will had consisted in large part of slaves. Though he felt affection for some of his slaves and spoke at one point of the "iniquity of slavery in the abstract,"[19] his correspondence on plantation affairs with Thomas Percy demonstrates that he regarded his Negroes primarily as chattel, to be cared for and treated with consideration and kindness because such treatment was economically sound. Since a large part of his investment was tied up in slaves, it was his good fortune that their price did not reflect the general downward trend other property had followed since the panic of 1819.[20]

Percy, in his capacity as caretaker of Oakland, often wrote Walker about what he called "Walker's people."

Thus, Percy sold "Sam and his wife for [$]1000 in notes," on November 16, 1819 and planned to dispose of Polydare the next day. Plymouth, on the other hand, had proved a dead weight; "his legs will hang him," Percy declared, and the market was not for him.[21] Early in 1820, Louisa, running to meet her husband upon his arrival from Georgia, slipped and fell. Premature labor resulted, and, although the child was born alive, it was not expected to survive another day.[22] On another occasion Percy wrote that Nancy was ill, but that she was getting the best diet and treatment possible, and "with the assistance of buttermilk and other nutritious beverages of that sort she may be worth looking at in the spring."[23] From time to time Percy reminded Walker that the slaves were part of "the family circle," and their master could thank God that all were well.[24] And when at length Percy made an Eastern trip, he looked upon the slave country thereafter with increased satisfaction, reporting that the people there were better off than they were in the North "with all their freedom."[25]

Such opinion notwithstanding, slavery continued to "ingulph everything" within the Congress. A seemingly endless series of motions concerned with the subject occupied the Senate's days, Walker and William Rufus King of Alabama voting consistently with the pro-slavery group. A motion which would have admitted Maine to the Union independently of Missouri was defeated 25 to 18 on January 14. Two weeks later a measure prohibiting the further introduction of slavery into Missouri fell, 27 to 16.[26] A fortnight later the Senate accepted, 23 to 21, the report of its Judiciary Committee uniting the Maine and Missouri statehood bills.[27] Three affirmative votes cast by Southern-born senators, Ninian Edwards and Jesse B. Thomas of Illinois and Waller Taylor of Indiana, aided the Southern men to secure passage of this.

One day later, on February 17, Senator Thomas introduced a measure providing for the exclusion of slavery in all that portion of the Louisiana Purchase lying north of the parallel of 36° 30′, except for Missouri. Under the Thomas amendment, "involuntary servitude" could be used to punish crime, and all escaped persons "from whom labor or service is lawfully claimed in any state or territory," would be returned. Thus amended, the joint Maine-Missouri bill rode to a third reading by a vote of 24 to 20. Glover Moore observes that this "bill embraced all of the compromise measures [and] a vote for engrossment was a vote for the compromise."[28] But the House refused to approve, and when the measure was returned to the upper chamber, the Senate voted 23 to 21 to stand firm by the Thomas amendment. Walker's and King's votes provided the margin of victory. Then by a vote of 11 to 33 the Senate refused to recede from the amendments prohibiting the further introduction of slavery into the United States territory north of 36° 30'.[29] After the House twice rejected the Senate's amendments, a joint committee was appointed in an attempt to reach a compromise.[30]

"When in Gods name will you finish this cursed Missouri question?" Tom Percy demanded of his brother-in-law. "You do nothing while that is pending. I heartily wished your great men were all tongue-tied upon it and forced to vote it fairly over at once."[31] Many people shared his views.

Walker had foreseen that the Senate would reject all restrictions on Missouri's admission as a state, but the vote was close. He felt that the amendment coupling Missouri and Maine was the means "which can save us" and wrote Tait that he had believed all along the question would be compromised and that "a law should pass forbidding the introduction of slavery in the territory of the U.S. north of some latitude—say 38°."[32] But for some, at least, compromise was no answer. Nathaniel Macon felt that "to compromise is to acknowledge the right of Congress to interfere and to legislate on the subject, this would be acknowledging too much.[33] Macon was delighted by the Washington rumor that members of the Virginia Legislature had urged congressmen to refrain from any compromise.

To Walker, a compromise would soothe discord—a highly desirable eventuality. He discovered that many "ardent annectionists" favored compromise until the arrival of King of New York, when "these humanity-men" found "their consciences . . . awakened and forbid them to tolerate such a damning sin. . . . This cunning man," wrote Walker, thought he had the pro-slavery advocates "in the toils. . . . He thinks to seat himself in the presidential chair" through the creation of a new party which would "swallow up all others." All distinctions between Federalists and Republicans, "all modifications of party, in short, growing out of speculation and opinions in relation to national policy in the administration of the government according to certain systems, are to be done away—and we are to have slave-holders, and non-slaveholders."

King was the arch fiend. King and his colleagues planned to capture Pennsylvania and then Ohio, in which case, he could exclaim "woe unto James 2! and woe unto us of the South! we shall have a slave holding President no more. . . . He has sailed the tempest which threatens the peace and existence of this Union, merely to ride on it into power," Walker wrote Tait.[34] When King was re-elected to the Senate, half of his object had been achieved, in Walker's opinion. Now he was working on the other half. But he would fail eventually. "I shall not be at all surprised if that other arch intriguer and potent politician, DeWitt [Clinton], should out reach him. And it is to be hoped that while they are quarrelling, we may save the Republic."[35]

Walker's appraisal of the New York political battle was shrewd. Governor DeWitt Clinton, a nominal Democrat, had accepted Federalist support in his efforts to defeat Madison for the Presidency in 1812, and the stigma of unorthodoxy continued to follow him. In 1820 he was still not in the good graces of the administration. Apparently motivated by a desire to embarrass his Tammany Hall, intra-Democratic opposition in New York, Clinton threw himself into the campaign against expansion of slavery into Missouri. In the gubernatorial election of 1820, Vice-President Daniel D. Tompkins, the Tammany candidate, opposed Clinton, and surprisingly enough was supported by King, despite Clinton's repeated charges that Tompkins was pro-Southern because of his stand on the Missouri issue. King's efforts notwithstanding, Clinton won an uneasy victory, and raised the spectre of a rejuvenation of the Federalist Party in the minds of many Northern Democrats. Reappearance of this perennial ghost helped to assuage some part of the sectional bitterness rife in the Congress.[36]

Meanwhile King continued his campaign for re-election to the Senate. Walker observed that in one address on February 11 he "emancipated the whole of our slaves by one potent *ipso dixit*." "The law of nature—that is the law of God—that is the Christian dispensation—forbids Slavery," King reportedly said. King reasoned, according to Walker, that the law of God is superior to the law of man, and therefore no human compact could establish or tolerate slavery. By such reasoning, Walker commented, "all our Southern Constitutions are of the devil's own making" and their slavery provisions were nullified by a higher law.[37] An ironic twist in the anti-slavery position, causing Walker an acrid amusement, hinged on Southern representation in the Congress. "They cannot consent that any more negro-representatives . . . sit in the Congress"; the South under the three-fifths compromise already had too much power in the eye of the free-state men. But if their policy were adopted, "they will abolish slavery and give us the whole ⅗th"—an obvious logical absurdity.

Though Walker expressed his opinion privately time and again, and "often felt strongly impelled to enter the arena," he did not speak on the Missouri question. The Southern argument had "been most ably sustained" in his opinion, particularly by William Pinkney of Maryland and James Barbour of Virginia.[38] Later, he was glad of his restraint, feeling that it enabled him "to do more good" by pouring oil on troubled waters.[39] But political associates, friends, and relatives in Alabama felt no such reluctance. Tait predicted dire consequences in a letter to Congressman Thomas W. Cobb. The Missouri question had become entangled with emancipation, a question intimately connected with Southern property rights, "with our social repose, with our safety." He held that if Congress should insist on interfering with salvery, "the Slave holding States must and no doubt will form a Separate Confederacy for themselves." He recommended as his strategy that Missouri refuse to enter the Union under a restriction on slavery; when she had 60,000 inhabitants, he felt she could demand admission almost upon her own terms.[40]

Thomas Percy had suggested this same plan to Walker.[41] He had prayed that Congress would admit Missouri with "an unshackled and constitutional government." Should it persist in its refusal to do so, however, he hoped the area would "patiently endure a Territorial government," until the next census, when he felt her population would be great enough to enable her to demand admission and receive it on terms granting her "equal rights with the other states."

On March 2 a House bill for admitting Missouri with restriction on the admission of slaves into the state was read by the House Clerk and presented to the Senate. Senator Barbour offered an amendment to strike out the restrictionist clause, and the Senate voted approval, 27 to 15. Senator Thomas again presented his amendment, and it was adopted without a recorded vote.[42] Thus amended, the bill was returned to the House. The same day the House heard the Joint Conference Committee's report, which recommended: (1) that the Senate withdraw its amendments to the Maine bill; (2) that both houses strike the slavery restriction clause from the House Missouri bill; and (3) that an amendment be added to the House Missouri bill excluding slavery from the Louisiana Territory north of parallel 36° 30', except Missouri.

The House was induced to concur by means of Henry Clay's adroit maneuvering and a break in the solidarity of the Northern votes, some of the representatives voting with the Southerners. The Senate, of course, gave its approval without difficulty. On March 3, 1820 the Senate removed its amendments to the Maine bill, the debate ended, and the free state was admitted to the Union. By an act of March 6 the second and third provisions of the compromise became law and the people of Missouri were authorized to write a constitution. The Missouri debate appeared to be settled.[43]

Walker expressed his "satisfaction" with the compromise. "It was a wild and necessary occasion," he told Tait,[44] "and has saved the Republic." Tait was inclined to attribute the achievement to the Senate's firmness, proclaiming that "future generations will rise up and call it *blessed.*"[45] He reported that the settlement had met with passive approval in Alabama. Personally, he would have preferred "a full and intire victory," but under the circumstances perhaps the best possible course had been taken. The President and the Southern senators would "take care for the future how Treaties are formed with the Indian Tribes west [and] north of the proposed state of Missouri [and by this means] the point in the compromise surrendered by the South may become mostly nominal."[46] Tait may well have touched upon the strategy which induced a number of Southerners to approve the bill—a silent, undercover agreement as to the course of action in the future.

It was a blow to Walker when the Missouri question erupted again six months later. The proposed Missouri Constitution contained a provision empowering the State Legislature to prohibit free Negroes and mulattoes from entering the state. The "instrument contains some foolish and unnecessary clauses, which will cause trouble," Walker reported. He feared Missouri would not be admitted, knowing the climate in the House, but he hoped the restrictionists would keep their promise to "give their decision without debate. When conviction is not to be hoped for, discussion merely inflates and *inveterates*," he wrote.[47] Tait prayed the issue would not be revived again, foreseeing that it would consume much of the session and perhaps "leave a bitterness of feeling very unfriendly to the continuance of our Union."[48] Revived it was, however. Tom Percy wrote that he hesitated to mention Missouri to Walker, for he realized that Walker was "sick with the mere name. Heaven send us a deliverance from this baleful contest & the devil take the fiend who hatched it," said Percy.[49]

As the new phase of the battle dragged on, John C. Calhoun came to hold views much closer to those of Walker and Tait. "I do not in the least doubt," he wrote Tait,[50] "but that the Missouri question was got up by a few designing politicians in order to extend their influence and power. [The question is] of the most mischievous character, being such as was well calculated to alienate the affections

of the people of one section from the other and to destroy
that unit of sympathy which makes us one people." However, it would be a great mistake to infer, he felt, that "as
the politicians were sustained by the North on the Missouri
question, the people in that quarter entered into their
views, or that even the leaders were actuated by a hatred to
the South, rather than a restless ambition."[51] Calhoun
seemed to be comforted by his belief that no conspiracy to
dissolve the Union existed. Walker and Tait, on the other
hand, feared that the hatred engendered by the crisis and
the action which might be precipitated could well lead to
disunion regardless of the basic motives underlying the
dispute.[52]

In December hostilities ceased for a time while the issue
was suspended between the two houses.[53] With the New
Year, Walker looked at the approach of adjournment and
surmised that the possible consequences of refusing to
admit the state would begin to have some effect. "They
admit that Missouri is no longer a Territory. They must,
then be a State; and if not a State of this Union, then
independent of it. What then becomes of the public lands
and all our national rights in Missouri? . . . Does civil
war exist?" he asked.[54] Would the gentlemen of the Congress intervene by force?

Walker and King continued to vote with the great
majority of their Southern colleagues on the issue. After an
unsuccessful attempt, an amendment was passed with their
aid which they hoped would mollify the opposition. Nothing in the action of Congress, this amendment provided,
was to be construed as an assent to any provision in the
Missouri Constitution contravening "that clause in the
U.S. constitution which declares that 'the citizens of each

state shall be entitled to all privileges and immunities of
citizens in the several states.' " A subsequent effort to
remove this amendment was defeated 27 to 17.[55] The
following day the entire admission resolution passed the
Senate by a vote of 26 to 18. Nathaniel Macon of North
Carolina was the sole Southern opponent, while the senators from Maine and Illinois, Senator Waller Taylor of
Indiana, and the Democrat John Parrott of New Hamp-
shire joined the majority.[56]

In the House it was a different matter. With the greater
strength of the North and East in that chamber, repeated
votes and fierce debate failed to attain an acceptable
modification of the Senate's admission bill.[57] Toward the
end of February, Clay, with the assistance of renewed fears
of Federalist rejuvenation, pushed through a compromise.
Under it, Missouri would agree never to deprive citizens of
another state of the privileges and immunities granted
them under the United States Constitution. Congress
accepted this as the formula; in June, Missouri agreed to
this moral pledge; in August, the President proclaimed her
admission to statehood.[58]

To Walker and almost every one else, a surcease to this
divisive quarrel was welcome, no matter how insecure the
solution. As the *Alabama Republican* had observed "[For]
two years this subject has embarrassed the proceedings of
Congress, prolonged the first session [of the Sixteenth
Congress] to an unprecedented extent, and obstructed the
passage of many wholesome and necessary laws [in the
second session]. No step can be taken but this question, like
Hamlet's Ghost, will arise to retard progress." On the appropriation bill, in memorializing Congress on the subject
of land relief, in counting the votes in the electoral college,
Missouri had presented itself.[59] Now the great issue di-

viding the nation had been settled, at least for a time, by compromise. Walker and his Southern colleagues could take pride in the fact that, if they had not won, they had at least prevented any greater damage to their interests.

EIGHT

Expansion to the South

WHILE WALKER AND HIS COLLEAGUES IN THE CONGRESS struggled over Missouri, the Administration was forced to cope with a second vexing controversy. Monroe and his Cabinet, during Walker's first months in Washington, viewed a dispute with Spain over the acquisition of Florida as one of its most troublesome problems—perhaps a transcendent one, since from time to time it threatened to explode into war. A tyro in the area of international diplomacy, the United States had perforce to determine a foreign policy in the hectic climate of an emergency. John Williams Walker, freshman Senator, became entangled in the Florida affair partially because Alabama coveted all Florida territory west of the Appalachicola River and had memorialized Congress to this effect in her Constitutional Convention.[1]

The Florida dispute was far from new in 1819 when Walker took his Senate seat. As early as 1805, Jefferson had asked Congress for a $2,000,000 appropriation to aid him in negotiations for West Florida. Though Jefferson's efforts were fruitless, by 1813 a rebellion and military occupation had combined to gain for the United States the land west of the Perdido River. In the ensuing five years, Spanish strength declined as rapidly as American nationalism—and with it, demands for Florida—increased. At length, in 1817, a rejuvenation of the 1808 revolutions in the Spanish American colonies provoked a change in Spanish strategy. Now, Spain conceded that the United States could have Florida if she would refuse to recognize any of the rebellious colonies. To achieve this goal, Don Luis de Onis Y Gonzales, Spanish minister to the United States, began negotiations for a treaty in early 1818. But it was at this point that Andrew Jackson entered the story.

Commissioned by the United States late in 1817 to punish the Seminoles, who had been raiding American territory and providing a haven for escaped slaves, Jackson was authorized to pursue them across the Spanish border if necessary. But Jackson, with characteristic intensity, moved into Florida; seized St. Marks and Pensacola; tried and executed two British citizens; deposed the Spanish governor, naming an American in his place; and burned the Spanish archives.[2]

Onis demanded a return of Florida to Spanish authority, a money indemnity for the episode, and punishment of Jackson. Yet he continued to negotiate with Secretary of State John Quincy Adams over the treaty, assuming that Florida would be restored.[3] Meantime opinions of Jackson's precipitate action began to circulate. American officialdom was appalled and apprehensive.

In an exchange of letters between Secretary of War John C. Calhoun and his friend Charles Tait,[4] Calhoun called the act "unauthorized, and done by Jackson on his own responsibility." He indicated the captured area would, of course, be returned to Spain and almost at any cost, war would be avoided.

We have nothing to gain in a Spanish war and much to lose. Should the contest be confined to Spain and us, our

commerce must pass from us to the neutral powers, particularly England. Should other powers be involved, and
the war general, the wisest man cannot see its result. We
must suffer. We want Time. Let us grow.[5]

To this Tait made a reply expressing at least partial
agreement, since somewhat later he mirrored Calhoun's
opinion when advising Walker on the Florida dispute.
Calhoun, greatly concerned over any such provocative
action as Jackson's, wrote again:

> Your train of reflections in relation to Jackson and Pensa-
> cola is such as I expected. . . . It is indispensable that the
> military should on all occasions be held subordinate to
> orders; and, I know of no excuses except necessity that
> ought to exempt from punishment disobedience to orders.
> . . . I have spoken to you freely on this interesting sub-
> ject. You will consider it between ourselves.[6]

But on the Administration's failure to punish Jackson,
Calhoun hedged. "Adversity of opinion, as to the character
of his [Jackson's] conduct" kept the Cabinet from recommending court-martial, he declared. Some held that the
General had acted under orders from the President—orders
which Jackson had interpreted as authority to take the
action he had taken.

> When to this was added the misconduct of the Spanish
> authority in Florida and the relation of this country with
> Spain, it was thought it would be highly improper to
> order any proceedings against the General. . . . Such
> was the diversity of view taken on this subject [that it
> would] render it, perhaps, improper, to take the high
> toned course; as that ought not to be resorted to but in a
> case free from doubt.[7]

Alabama politicians, who looked upon Jackson's growing
political strength with misgivings, were less placatory.

Governor W. W. Bibb wrote Tait that in apologizing for General Jackson the government had erred most egregiously. He maintained that nothing would be gained with Jackson's friends, and, at the same time, the government leaders would

> . . . lose much with the thinking part of the Nation. Not a moment should have been lost in arresting the Genl. and thereby showing a just regard to the preservation of our constitution. No man should be permitted in a free country to usurp the whole powers of the whole government and to treat with contempt all authority except that of his own will.[8]

Secretary of the Treasury William H. Crawford concurred. In the Cabinet dispute over the fiasco, Crawford had supported "investigation by a military tribunal;—in other words, court martial."[9] Already a leading presidential candidate, Crawford perhaps saw Jackson as peculiarly menacing to his ambitions, though he professed to discount the General's political strength.[10] "What ought to be done with this Man?" Crawford asked. "He is not inferior to the Georgia Genl. [John Clark] in depravity and vindictiveness, and superior to him in talents and address."[11]

Georgia Congressman Thomas W. Cobb, as late as 1822, deplored the fact that the affair was never properly exploited. Cobb saw Georgia's Governor John Clark, Calhoun, and Jackson as a political triumvirate dedicated to defeating Crawford's presidential aspirations. "A glorious chance to dissolve this confederacy has been lost," he declared. Had wisdom guided the investigations of "the late Florida transactions Jackson would have been ruined."[12]

Walker, surrounded by antagonism to Jackson, was never in full accord with his associates on the subject. He enjoyed a close friendship with General John Coffee, who was Jackson's nephew-in-law and intimate friend. He was indebted to Jackson for recommending him for political appointment, and it was not in Walker's nature to forget a debt of this kind. Moreover, with his political acumen, he could not help but feel the pressure of the popular following Jackson was amassing in Alabama as well as elsewhere.[13]

Secretary of State Adams chose to defend Jackson, in effect contending that "Spain must either exercise responsible authority in the derelict province or cede it to the United States." And with this warning, he returned Florida to Spain. Shortly thereafter, the new Spanish foreign minister instructed Onis to grant Florida to the United States and to settle the "whole territorial question as best he could, preferably by running the [western] boundary along the Missouri to its source and thence to the ocean *as far north as possible*."

Onis received this carte blanche on January 4, 1819. On February 22, he formally signed the Adams-Onis Treaty, ceding Florida to the United States and fixing a transcontinental boundary line between the United States and Spanish territory west of the Mississippi River. Two days later, the Senate by unanimous consent, ratified the treaty.[14] The Florida dispute appeared to be settled.

But as Walker prepared to take his position in the Senate, the document reached Madrid, where it was unexpectedly repudiated. The Spanish Council of State, reviewing the treaty for King Ferdinand, pointed out that it contained no guarantee that the United States would not recognize the independence of the Latin American states. It contained no promise that the United States would enforce its neutrality laws more effectively. And in the

Council's opinion, it ceded far too much territory. King Ferdinand appointed a new emissary, General Don Francisco Dionisio Vives, with instructions to embark for Washington where he would re-open the negotiations.

As time passed, an impatient American public bent on expansion clamored for action, and Walker watched government officials in Washington react alarmingly. Secretary Adams urged Monroe to advise Congress to occupy the Floridas by force. Henry Clay, jubilant because he felt that Spain had saved the country from an unprofitable deal, demanded from the House that the United States occupy both Florida and Texas.[15] Crawford wrote Tait in November that there was no intention of making Spain's refusal to ratify the treaty a cause of war. He believed that the course pursued would be to occupy the Floridas and issue at the same time a declaration stating that "we shall limit our views to the accomplishment of what Spain ought to have done for us." He felt that by this means war might be avoided.[16]

Inevitably, Walker had the advice of Judge Charles Tait. Echoing Calhoun, Tait said he feared a war would be "disastrous" to the United States since its navigation would be sacrificed and its commerce would be prey to privateering interests. The American navy was much too small, and even at ten times its present strength could hardly protect American shipping.[17]

He knew, he said, that Florida speculators would exert great pressure for war—"all persons who expect contracts and fat jobs; all the military by land and sea who honestly pant for action and an opportunity to distinguish themselves"—but, did these special groups represent "the interest of the nation?" Having reviewed with care the arguments against a declared war, Tait recommended that the United States occupy "as much of Florida as may be necessary to secure us against Indian depradation." Once this was done, negotiation could go forward "on a solid basis," since the United States would have "one foot on Florida and the other on Texas bestriding the Gulf of Mexico."[18]

While Walker agreed that war with Spain might annihilate American commerce, he feared that a state of hostilities—an undeclared war—might easily grow out of the measures adopted, and might be equally damaging.[19] On the same day that he was seated in the Senate, December 7, 1819, President Monroe, in his annual State of the Union message, asked Congress for authority to take over Florida. Walker, pondering the result of any attempt to execute the President's policy, decided that if it were acted upon, there would certainly have to be qualifications. Perhaps a time would be set for Spanish concurrence "beyond which no explanation will be allowed, no grace accorded." Meanwhile one could only wait and hope.[20] Though the House Committee on Foreign Affairs reported a bill in response to the President's request, it and a number of proposed amendments were successfully bottled up.[21]

Three months later, Adams advised the President to send a special message suggesting that Congress delay action on his recommendations until the next session, so that sufficient time would elapse for a new Spanish minister to arrive. Meanwhile, the Georgia leader, John Forsyth, was appointed the new United States minister to Spain, and Adams instructed him that if Spain withheld approval of the Adams-Onis Treaty, "the United States would insist upon further indemnity, and would reassert and never again relinquish its rights to a western boundary at the Rio Grande del Norte."[22]

Forsyth's mission proved notably unsuccessful and brought upon him the wrath and disapproval of his former colleagues. Israel Pickens wrote Walker that Forsyth might have achieved better results if he had "used a little more of the *suaviter in modo,* and left the *fortiter* to the government at home."[23] Judge Tait commented that Forsyth had permitted himself "to depart from the usual style, and temper, and courtesy in Diplomatic affairs." In an obvious reference to Jackson, he asked, "sh. not the same rule be applied to the man who runs riot in civil matters as to him who violates all Laws in Military affairs?" He hoped that Forsyth would be permitted "to go off even with *eclat* in consideration first that he has only bullied Spain and second because his motive was good."[24] But on second thought, Tait came to feel that Forsyth should be called home at once, since he could do no possible good in Madrid. He had "subjected himself to the imputation of hunting for popularity through his diplomatic agency."[25] Forsyth returned to Washington, and Walker, at least, was convinced that he had been recalled.

On April 9, 1820, King Ferdinand's new emissary, General Vives, arrived. Walker reported a series of rumors flooding the capital. First, he had brought the ratified treaty in his pocket. Six days later he had not brought the treaty. Next, he had been authorized to agree to a new treaty which would permit the "instant possession of the Floridas" by the United States upon its concurrence.[26] General Vives in due course made known Spain's actual demands for ratification: The United States must strengthen her neutrality laws; guarantee Spain's possessions in the western hemisphere; and pledge no recognition of the independence of any of the Spanish-American colonies in revolt. These Secretary Adams flatly refused, holding that the United States had pursued a neutral policy, and that to give pledges never to recognize the independence of the rebellious colonies would be a violation of neutrality.[27]

By this time Walker had no fear that Congress would declare war. "No body is mad enough just now to fight for Florida," he wrote. "Our *sinews* are unstrung. Our war-chest is as empty as an exhausted receiver. The treasury . . . is *minus* even for the peace establishment." In such circumstances, the United States would not precipitate a war.[28] But at the close of the session in May, Walker bemoaned the fact that no major developments had taken place on the Florida issue. Not only had the nation not taken Florida; it had not rested "authority in the President to do so contingently. 'Our poverty, and not our will, consents,' " Walker wrote shortly before he left for Alabama.[29]

General Vives' departure from Madrid had preceded by a brief interval a liberal revolution in Spain. Once again events in Europe had transpired to relieve the diplomacy of the United States. The revolution, together with the danger that the United States might seize Florida—and even Texas, should Henry Clay's views prevail—led to a reversal of policy. With Spain now isolated in Europe and threatened in America, the Spanish Council of State urged ratification, and the "new constitutional" Cortes gave its approval in secret on September 30, 1820, at the same time annulling its Florida land grants. King Ferdinand signed the treaty October 24, 1820.[30]

Secretary of War Calhoun believed that only the revolution in Spain had diverted inevitable American occupation of Florida. "There would have been little, or no diversity as to the course to be pursued on the termination of the correspondence with General Vives: the occupation of the country in dispute would have followed," he wrote.[31]

When Congress reconvened in the fall of 1820, no official papers on the ratification had been received by the American government, though rumors that the cession had been accomplished were repeated in the London journals and in private letters from Madrid.[32] Not until January, 1821, were all doubts dispelled "of its approval by the King with advice and consent of the Cortez."[33] And even then, President Monroe was forced to place the treaty's fate once again in the hands of the Senate, because the original agreement had provided that ratification must be exchanged within six months. Walker expressed fear that "unctious politicians, [who] look with more solicitude to Texas" than to Florida, might impede its progress, a fear which proved unfounded. On February 19, 1821, the Senate gave its approval,[34] and Walker could turn his attention to securing for Alabama the territory in Florida which she coveted.

The memorial to Congress written in Alabama's Constitutional Convention prayed that, upon the ratification of the treaty of annexation, that portion of Florida lying west of the Appalachicola River be added to Alabama.[35] Much of this area, the memorial pointed out, lay along the southern border of Alabama; Pensacola, it continued, "must become" the main seaport for at least the portion of the state "which lies south of [the] chain of Mountains dividing the waters of the Tennessee River from that of Mobile Bay." Unless the area should be given to Alabama, it held, two-thirds of Alabama "will be blocked by a strip of territory 50 miles in breadth." Furthermore, this portion of Florida was held to be composed of barren soil, while eastern Florida "appears of itself sufficiently extensive to form a state." The memorial requested Congress to examine the condition of all concerned. If Congress acted after such an investigation, the Convention had no fear as to the ultimate results.[36]

Judge Tait was, as a matter of course, eager to see Congress comply with the request of the Convention. "Our Geographical symmetry will be marred unless this annexation takes place," he declared. It was his hope that "the local divisions of this State, our northern and our southern interest, will not operate to obstruct a measure which cannot but be for the interest of this community."[37]

Walker let no grass grow under his feet. The Senate had scarcely cast the last vote in approval of the treaty when Senator Walker of Alabama presented the memorial of his state's Convention. It was promptly referred to the Foreign Relations Committee, and shortly thereafter the Committee was discharged from the consideration of the measure on a motion of Senator James Barbour of Virginia.[38] Ill-fated from the beginning, Alabama's plea languished, although neither Alabamians nor their representative in the Senate gave up hope. A full year later, Judge Tait was still sanguine. He wrote Walker anticipating possible rearrangement of his court sessions should West Florida be added to his district. Since Pensacola was "as healthy in September as in January," he contemplated retreating to the coast during the "sickly season" in South Alabama. He hoped the annexation would take place, since he judged it "necessary for them and for us."[39]

In July, 1822, nearly eighteen months after ratification, Walker was asked by J. H. Chaplin, a Floridian desiring

Alabama annexation, when a new memorial should be sent to Congress from the residents of Pensacola. Chaplin reported that when he had presented a memorial a year earlier "the measure was unpopular," and he had been able to obtain only about 230 signatures, but he was convinced that three-fourths "are now in favor" of annexation to Alabama. He wondered if it would be wiser to memorialize the next session or to delay yet another session before again petitioning Congress.[40]

During the intervening year, the Senate had passed a bill establishing a territorial government for Florida, and when the measure was under debate, Walker had offered an amendment providing for the annexation of West Florida to Alabama.[41] The amendment was defeated 25 to 19, Walker, William R. King, William Smith of South Carolina, and Thomas H. Williams of Mississippi constituting its only Southern supporters.[42] Walker had "made sundry eloquent languages" on the subject and felt that he had demonstrated that the annexation would be best for both Florida and Alabama. Though he received "a great many very fine compliments" on his efforts, he could not muster the necessary votes. Seeking an explanation, Walker wrote Tait, "It failed chiefly from the fears of the South." But he believed the failure was temporary. "It must finally succeed. The County belongs to us by position and common interests. Nature has given it to us, and Congress will not always withhold [it]"—an opinion Walker found three-fourths of the Senate concurred in. The peninsula was "competent of itself" to become a state, and once this fact became apparent, "the natural union of West Florida and Alabama will [be] no longer forbidden."[43]

The Florida affair had its dénouement. On March 8, 1822, Monroe sent a message to Congress advocating recognition of the independence of the Latin American republics, and Congress complied, in spite of the strong protests of the Spanish minister. Walker felt that threats of Spanish reprisals would come to nought and her actions would be confined to words. He was content to close the dispute with a wry comment. "Less *sensation* has been excited by this measure than you would imagine," he wrote. "Many *great-men,* it is said, are ready and willing to visit these new powers in quality of ambassadors etc."[44]

Within a few weeks, the independent republics had received American recognition, and the Florida episode was at an end.

NINE

Domestic Legislation

DURING JOHN WILLIAMS WALKER'S BRIEF TENURE IN THE Senate, the nation was beset by severe economic depression. Congress struggled with measures allegedly designed to alleviate distress—a national bankruptcy bill and a protective tariff among them. The bankruptcy bill was one of frequent abortive attempts to provide legislation on the subject in compliance with the Constitution, which reserved to the Congress the right to establish uniform laws on bankruptcy.[1]

His own fortune threatened,[2] Walker was well aware of the suffering and deprivation everywhere. Larkin Newby, for example, was forced by business failure to sell all his property. "My wife and myself both feel more reluctance at parting with our Negroes, than all the rest of our property," he wrote Walker. He pointed out that his slaves consisted of two women and their children, all "born in this family and petted and spoiled almost as much as our own."[3] With such bitter personal experience to fortify his opinions, Newby took occasion to write Walker at length about the bankruptcy legislation, though he displayed little understanding of it. He expressed the opinion that a bankruptcy law, if founded on the principle of "a surrender of property for the benefit of *all creditors* would operate to the injury of our monied aristocracies—the Banks." Newby believed that "the interests of the *Banks* and of the *People* . . . [are] incompatible with each other. [As] one brot. up in a Compting house and who has felt the benefit of Banks," he held that banks were very useful "within proper limits, but extended as they have been and still are in our Country, with their almost unlimited *accommodation* loans, they are the veriest curse that ever befell our happy country!" He had always opposed their wide extension in the South and West and the monopoly the United States Bank enjoyed in the North.[4] Banks, he declared, nurtured "monied aristocracies . . . more to be dreaded in this country than all others." He reasoned that they would use their influence to stifle any bankruptcy legislation,[5] but as it turned out, the strongest congressional support for such legislation came from the Northern and Eastern states where support for a national bank was also greatest.

Walker wrote Newby that he was correct in assuming the law would require the debtor to "surrender for the benefit of *all* his creditors, without exception." There was, he declared, much to be said for and against such a measure. He personally entertained some doubts as to whether it "ought to pass."[6]

Judge Tait urged Walker to support the bankruptcy measure. Tait was in no circumstances to benefit from the law, and felt no qualms about freely expressing his opinion. To be effective, it would have to be retroactive in operation, he held. If a destitute person "surrenders to those by whom he is trusted everything he possesses and everything which induced the credit, can the person trusting have a *vested* right to any thing more?" Tait asked. Under laws then current, the debtor's future acquisitions could be taken by his creditors, but in the Judge's opinion, state legislatures clearly had the right to protect a man against such seizures. He recalled that the most common objection to a national bankruptcy law was that it opened the door to frauds, but he felt "that more frauds are committed in one year under an insolvent system, than in three under a bankrupt system. A man's duty to his loved ones, and securing some of his after-acquisitions to them is no fraud," Judge Tait declared.[7]

It is apparent from the record of his voting in the Senate that Walker had no use for the bankruptcy law, at least as written in 1820. On March 16, he and King joined with twelve other Senators in an unsuccessful effort to get the measure indefinitely postponed, and in a subsequent move to have it postponed until the next session. His voting on some of the proposed amendments indicates those features of the bill he found objectionable. For example, he supported an amendment to provide for voluntary bankruptcy. Introduced by Senator Nicholas Van Dyke, the amendment stated that a man in debt to any one creditor for as much as $1,000, or to two or more for $1,500 could become a voluntary bankrupt by presenting a petition to the judge of the court.[8] This amendment passed, 25 to 13, but on the following day a motion was made to strike it out and add another providing that debts of a bankrupt remaining unsatisfied under a bankrupt commission might be sued for as if no bankruptcy certificate had been issued. This was defeated, 24 to 18, with Walker's help.[9] He also helped defeat an amendment which would have exempted from the provisions of the law those "whose living is substantially gotten by mechanical labor, though with some mixture of buying and selling."[10]

After lengthy wrangling, the Senate voted to reject the

entire measure, and one day thereafter, upon a motion to reconsider, again defeated the bill, 17 to 19, Walker voting against it. The measure was dead for the current session.[11]

But the 16th Congress was far from through with bankruptcy. Resurrected promptly for the second session to handle, it was before the Senate on February 9, 1821, when Walker and King supported a motion to postpone its consideration indefinitely. The measure was defeated 32 to 10, whereupon the two Alabama senators sponsored a measure to recommit the bill to committee. This was also defeated, 24 to 13.[12]

Proposals for amendment followed each other interminably. One provided that if non-merchants or non-bankers committed any act "designated as that of bankruptcy," a judge, at the request of particular classes of creditors, might summon them before bankruptcy commissioners and force them to show cause why they should not be declared bankrupts. (Walker for, King against. Measure defeated.)[13] Another provided that no discharge be given "to any persons except those whose debts may be due to merchants, bankers, brokers, factors, underwriters, or marine insurers." (Walker for, King against. Measure defeated.)[14] A third, and vicious, proposal would have given bankruptcy commissioners authority to issue warrants to open for inspection any houses, chambers, or warehouses, owned by bankrupts. (Walker and King against. Measure defeated.)[15]

At this point the Senate voted on whether the entire bill should be engrossed and presented for a third reading. Both Walker and King voted against it, but the measure squeaked through, 19 to 18. On February 19, the vote on the third reading was 23 to 19 in the affirmative, both Alabama senators voting with the opposition.[16]

In the opinion of many debtors it was unfortunate that this measure was never enacted into law. It was defeated by a close vote in the House, March 1.[17] Walker's votes indicate that he opposed the legislation because he was essentially conservative and wanted to protect the rights of the creditor. But there was another reason for Southern opposition. Private planters, small farmers, and the like would not benefit. Only the intermediate capitalist stood to gain materially.

A new victim of the slump was the federal government, by nineteenth century standards grievously in debt. Inevitably the administration favored a national taxation policy. Inevitably Congress, with an eye to the constituents back home, opposed it. Walker received voluminous advice, though he scarcely needed it. Tait wrote late in 1819 when war with Spain threatened that the national debt was already large enough, but that war would raise it by, perhaps, some fifty or sixty million dollars and was therefore to be avoided, as was any system of internal taxation. As for the home front, "The good people of Alabama will have enough to do to pay our local debts and the debts we owe to the Genl. Govt.," he wrote. He estimated that Alabama people owed the banks one million dollars, "northern cities" one-half million, and the federal government, nine or ten million.[18] The outlook was bleak enough without new burdens.[19] A year later, the deficiency in the revenue of the federal government led him to think that expenditures must be cut or Congress would have to resort to new loans. He was confident that Congress would "hardly think of laying direct taxes at present. . . ."[20] The people of Alabama were in "no condition" to "pay Taxes." Their load was as great "as we can stagger along with for the next five or six years." He suggested that Congress would have "to lay its hands" on the surplus of the sinking fund and borrow, at least for the time being. "When the season of prosperity shall again come taxes may then be imposed, but at present that pressure with our other difficulties would grind us to dust."[21]

Walker was ready to support a program providing for "a small loan and a temporary division of so much of the sinking fund as is not required for the service of the year" if it were introduced.[22] But in the meantime a far more ominous measure was projected. With exquisite sarcasm Walker wrote Tait, "As a panacea for these hard times [it is proposed] to cut off some half a dozen millions of our revenue from imports by the establishment of a new tariff, [thus clipping] the wings of our commerce and naviga- tion and [accommodating] agriculture with a direct tax and sundry little indirect ditto . . . [and managing only] to propitiate the redoubtable Mr. Carey[23] and the manu- facturers." Firmly opposed, Walker anticipated a spirited contest when the measure came before the Senate.[24] But a minor skirmish in the protectionism war occupied the Senators first. In early April, 1820, a bill requiring that the army be clothed exclusively in "domestic manufactures" was introduced. Senator John Williams of Tennessee pro- posed on April 14 that the further consideration of the matter be indefinitely postponed, but despite Southern support, the motion was defeated 24 to 17. On April 15, a motion to amend provided that all army materials be domestically procured if goods "of the same kind and quality" as those of foreign manufacture could be obtained at the same price. Walker and King supported the new version of the bill, and it carried, 39 to 3.[25] Protectionism had won a small concession.

Walker's fears of impending trouble proved unjustified.

When the complete tariff bill came to a vote in the Senate on May 4, it was disposed of with dispatch. Senator Barbour of Virginia moved that its consideration be postponed until the next session. Though the motion carried, the vote was close, 22 to 21, Walker, King, and all but five Southern senators voting for postponement.[26] Walker apparently believed that the Alabama vote had determined this crucial victory, for he wrote that though the Senate had remained in session a month too long, Alabama had saved "the South—or rather Agriculture and Commerce in the matter of the new tariff." The danger was, he hoped, "pretty well over."[27]

In July, his antipathy to protectionism and the tariff was reinforced by a letter from a Philadelphia friend, John Gaillard, who reported businesses were pretty much at a standstill there. According to Gaillard, it was "generally admitted that the manufacturing interest is doing well and perhaps better than any other description of our fellow citizens," despite its mournful cries for aid, and this proved "the folly of Mr. Baldwin's[28] mammoth tarif [sic] of duties, and the impolity of altering a system adopted before its merits have had time to be tested by experience and before it shall have undergone those fluctuations which are frequently produced by causes of a temporary nature."[29]

The tariff did not again plague the South's congressmen while Walker was serving in the Senate. It had made a momentary appearance, and bowed out. Walker considered its exit something of a personal triumph, but on other matters he was to be far less successful.

Early Alabama statesmen confronted as a major economic goal the opening of new land to immigrants and the securing of relatively cheap means of transporting their goods to market. Federal sponsorship of internal improvements, if obtained without additional taxation, would spur the state's economy and at the same time aid in solving the transportation problem, an idea that Walker found as inviting as most other Alabamians, including the first Governor. In April, 1820, Governor Bibb asked Walker to find out whether any money was available in state allocations from the sale of federal lands within the Alabama borders. The State Legislature had appropriated $4,000 from such funds for the employment of an engineer to explore the state's rivers. Bibb wanted the money as soon as possible, because the engineer was urgently needed, and his work would take several years to complete. The Governor added that in his opinion the bridges which had been demolished along the routes between Alabama and Georgia should be replaced, also as quickly as possible.[30]

Six months later, Bibb's brother, who succeeded him, gave the idea fresh impetus by devoting much of his 1820 message to the subject of internal improvements, with the result that the Legislature passed a bill establishing a board to study the situation.[31] And in the fall of 1821, the Alabama Legislature memorialized the Congress, seeking federal aid for a waterway. The petition contended that if the waters of the Hiwassee, a principal branch of the Tennessee, and the Alabama were connected, "the distance then required for the produce of Tennessee to find a market on the sea board, would be reduced from nearly two thousand miles to New Orleans, to six or seven hundred to Mobile." Advantages would accrue to the agriculturists of areas as far north as western Virginia,[32] the memorial pointed out in an effort to stress the national aspect. When Governor Israel Pickens forwarded the memorial to Walker, he urged him to use his "prudence" to call the attention of the "General Government" to the proposed project so that "when any general system shall be undertaken, this may not escape notice as a conspicuous national object." The memorial was presented to the Senate, January 22, 1822, and was referred to the Committee on Roads and Canals. Unfortunately no action was ever taken on it.[33]

Walker had been interested in federally sponsored internal improvement for some years. A clause in the state's admission act which had particularly delighted him called for three per cent of the sale price of public lands to be employed within the state for internal improvements. State rivers, Walker felt, should be the first object for consideration.[34] Much credit was due Tait, who had sponsored the admission act, because he had urged federal support of internal improvements. Applauding what he called Tait's "noble and extended views," Walker noted his deep regret that

. . . the constitutional scruples of two successive Presidents . . . are likely so long to retard the free march of a policy so obviously calculated to increase, almost beyond computation, the national wealth, and to draw close the bands of our federal Compact. . . . [it would] have been better to have followed his [Monroe's] advice, and put the question beyond all doubt or scruple by an amendment to the Constitution. . . . the public sentiment is decidedly in favor of such an amendment; and little doubt can be entertained that the requisite number of states would give it their sanction. Why is it not originated somewhere?[35]

His wholehearted espousal of federally-sponsored improvements within a single state stopped short, however, at the Alabama boundary line. A year after writing this letter to Tait, he voted twice, unsuccessfully, to postpone indefinitely consideration of a bill providing for the appointment of commissioners to lay out roads and canals in another state. On May 9, 1820, he voted to postpone indefinitely consideration of a bill authorizing the appointment of commissioners to lay out a canal in Ohio.[36] Again, on January 11, 1821, he sponsored a motion to postpone indefinitely consideration of another bill authorizing commissioners to lay out a canal in Ohio. During the first session of the 17th Congress he twice voted, both times with the majority, to terminate aid for the maintenance of the Cumberland Road which ran from Cumberland, Maryland, to Wheeling, Virginia.[37]

Yet Walker told the Senate that he opposed the Ohio canal not because of "any constitutional scruples," but because he envisioned a federal project on a vast scale. "Such a work [as the Ohio Canal] ought not to be undertaken unless as a part of a great system of internal improvement," and this particular project was not "the point at which such a system ought to be commenced." He would lend his support only to a complete system of federally-sponsored improvements, adequately planned and financed. Although he believed such a project would make a great contribution to the well-being of Alabama and the nation, the administration and an appreciable number of his fellow legislators did not share his opinion.[38] It was not to come in his age.

On the whole, Walker's answer to economic crisis appears to have been retrenchment, yet not at the expense of the nation's defense. Upon entering the Senate in 1819, he was appointed to the Committee on the Militia and the Committee on Naval Affairs,[39] positions from which he could scrutinize military needs and help to bolster the armed forces where necessary. In 1820, the million dollar appropriation for the Navy went untouched, a fact which was gratifying to Walker. At the same time he deplored the impending House defeat of a bill to authorize "building a few small vessels, for the protection of the Mexican Gulph [sic]," and of another creating the rank of rear admiral. He consoled himself and Tait with the fact that no attempt had been made to tamper with the Navy Board, whose utility and importance he felt to be essential to naval operations.[40]

Walker and King aided in the modification of the 1820 military appropriations bill so as to increase the allocation to the Quartermaster's Department from $450,000 to $500,-000. (The vote was 24 to 18.) Walker also successfully sponsored legislation making applicable to all naval officers the condition that "no present, or emolument of any kind whatsoever" might be accepted from "any king, prince, or foreign state. . . ."

In 1821, Walker noted that the House had reduced the Army to 6,000 men and had "made terrible laws among the staff and appendages"—actions with which, he was sure, neither the military committees of the Senate, nor the entire chamber would concur. He conceded that substantial deductions might be made for current appropriations, but he felt the Senate would engraft important modifications on the measure when it emerged from the House. His optimism was misplaced. When the Senate's modifications went to the Conference Committee, no agreement could be reached, and in order to extricate themselves from a stalemate, the Senate moved to recede from its amendments. This it did, with Walker's support, by a vote of 17 to 16.[41] In this same year the Navy's appropriations were cut in half, from $1,000,000 to $500,000 annually.[42] In his bitter defeat, Walker held his tongue and shunned criticism of his colleagues, practical politics so dictating.

Discreet at all times in Washington, he confided his opinions of officialdom only to Tait, whom he trusted implicitly. It is clear from his letters that he had no admiration for Monroe, yet publicly he maintained a prudent silence. To Tait, he described a presidential message in 1821 as "plain and unambitious of ornaments, as usual, . . . remarkably free from any bold or responsible recommendation."[43] Such judicious reserve helped him with the Andrew Jackson problem, too. A number of his friends, men of the Georgia Faction, committed political suicide in attempting to thwart the General's ambitions. Walker, too astute to fall into this trap, privately confessed his apprehensions. "I fear we [Jackson and Walker] think too much alike about some things touching the Seminole," he wrote Tait. "I would to God they were undone. He [Jackson] is a great man with great defects. One cannot help loving or blaiming [sic] him. But I follow your exemplary course;—and perhaps go further; when I cannot praise I try to be silent."[44]

In the late winter of 1822, Congress disintegrated into an imbroglio over the approaching presidential election. Walker noted that partisanship was rife, that majorities could "readily be mustered against any one man, but none in his favor." Adams, Crawford, Calhoun, Clay, and Clinton all had their factions, but some of the candidates would have to break down or withdraw, since no one of the group could singly be elected. "It is this way only that the South can succeed," he wrote. "It can never run three candidates and win."[45] It is notable that Walker did not list Jackson as a potential candidate, but Crawford, the Georgia Faction's mentor, was also unimpressed at this time with the Jackson ground swell. He wrote Tait[46] that the nomination of Jackson by the Tennessee Legislature "can produce no effect whatever, unless it should affect the election of Colonel [John] Williams to the Senate. I am fearful that it was intended more for that purpose than any other. There is no other state in the Union that will take him for President."

From the Washington vantage, Walker evaluated the chances of each of the candidates. Vice-President Daniel D. Tompkins had been eliminated by the "demon of intemperance." Clinton, he felt, "must rise again from the dead," but since the man was "a great magician," he might accomplish the trick "unless a little more unanimity be found in the rank of his enemies." William Lowndes was not making much of a sensation. John Quincy Adams could hope for nothing from the South, and it would be well for him "if New England itself does not desert him in his hour of need." Massachusetts Federalists seemed to "abominate his finished oration" and were supposed to have "a hankering after a more youthful love." That love, in 1822, seemed to be Calhoun, and hopes were "built on Pennsylvania in his favor because his father once lived there!"

Maine seemed to be for Crawford, as were some of "the Staunch Republicans of Massachusetts." He had "perhaps the best chance for the South." Virginia was uncertain, and Clay had been wooing her. Yet Walker felt that Crawford would "unite . . . a greater number" in Maryland, Virginia, North Carolina, and Georgia than any other man.[47] Walker concluded that it was too early to predict anything. If Clay and Crawford should get together, the result might be that the Georgian would dominate. In short, he believed with "Dr. Doubty," that "things are uncertain." It was probable that "there will be no choice by the people, and of course that the final result will be made by the House of Representatives." In that case, Walker felt, any of the leading candidates might be elected.[48]

Walker was not to remain in Washington to watch the outcome of his appraisal of presidential politics, for ill health would force him to resign his Senate seat in November. At best, however, his predictions were hardly prophetic, since they were colored by his own high estimate of the Georgia Faction's strength.

TEN

The Good Earth

As Alabama's first Senator, John Williams Walker inevitably found his greatest problem to be land and the staggering debts its purchase had engendered. In the summer of 1820, the United States Public Land Office reported that of the $21,173,489.87 which would be due the federal government at the end of the year from purchasers of public lands, $11,220,685.55, or nearly 53 per cent, was due from the single state of Alabama.[1] The remaining 47 per cent was shared by the newer states among the 22 then existing. This debt was the more overwhelming because the panic of 1819 had driven commodity prices to new lows and the ensuing depression had drained the state of resources. Walker's greatest contribution as a Senator was to be his successful campaign to secure revision of the land laws.

Under the land policy then prevailing, enacted into law in 1800 and 1803, federal lands were usually sold by the section and half-section on a credit basis, purchasers being required to pay one-fourth down (within forty days) and the balance, with interest at six per cent, in annual installments by the end of the second, third and fourth years.[2] There is no doubt that such a system encouraged the rapid settlement of frontier land. On February 2, 1818, the

Government Land Office, recently installed at Huntsville, offered for sale for the first time Tennessee Valley lands outside the bounds of Madison County—lands about which "the most wonderful accounts of . . . fertility" had been circulated in the older states. Within a year, seven new counties had been created out of wilderness and nourished "flourishing villages" as their county seats "and a large and prosperous population within their borders."[3] But at the same time, such a system abetted land speculation of the wildest and most predatory nature. Even the individual settler was induced by it to purchase "just as much land as he could possibly cover on the first payment, hoping that he might be able to earn enough within the first credit period to meet the subsequent payments."[4] From its inception, the credit policy had proved too stringent for many purchasers, and their appeals had led Congress to pass eleven separate relief measures between 1806 and 1820, extending additional credit to various groups. In Walker's opinion such stopgap provisions would no longer be adequate. Only a complete change of the basic system would suffice. Furthermore, though speculation had played a major part in precipitating Alabama's plight, Congress and the "Mississippi Stock"[5] also bore a good share of responsibility. Four million dollars worth of this paper had been "thrown into the market at once and was bot [sic] up to a great extent at 45-50 and 60 per Centum,"[6] with immediate effect on land prices.

"I believe that it is generally understood that we here cannot pay for our lands if the present laws are enforced," Charles Tait wrote. "They must be generally forfeited." He advocated an extension of time for payment and the remission of back interest, reasoning that if the payments were divided into eight installments, with no interest charged until the day the installment was due, the great majority of purchasers would be able to meet their payments, and would do so rather than forfeit their lands. Tait urged Walker to lead the Congress in such a course.[7]

Walker was well aware of the critical nature of the land indebtedness in Alabama.[8] By 1820, settler and speculator alike were foundering. Early in the year, when a bill was reported from the Committee on Public Lands, the question of land policy was opened for general debate, and Walker went into action. The bill as reported called for disestablishment of the credit system and the reduction of the minimum price of lands from $2.00 to $1.25 an acre.[9] On February 22, Walker moved to amend it to provide that purchasers of public lands be privileged to relinquish their lands for resale before the new law went into operation. Under his proposal, the government would then sell the land in the same manner as it sold all forfeited land, "but, if such lands shall sell for more than one dollar and _____ cents per acre, the excess shall be paid over to the former certificate holder," provided that this excess did not exceed the amount the purchaser had already paid the United States.[10] Having presented his amendment, he spoke at length in its defense, pointing out that the practical effect of the system then being used was to give purchasers, by indulgences, an almost indefinite period of time for repayment. Some lands purchased in Ohio more than twenty years before were still unpaid for. Moreover, the amount owed the federal government for lands was over $22,000,000—"a fearful sum."

Walker's object, he declared, was ultimately to change the law which produced such results, but if a radical change were made too suddenly, the price of lands would fall so disastrously as to prejudice the interest of current holders. The most recent purchasers would suffer the greatest loss because in many cases they had paid actual value in their first installment. He argued that any new law should protect these people from the depreciation which would result from its passage—a protection assured by his amendment.

To forestall an objection he knew would be raised, Walker confessed that some speculators would undoubtedly profit, but there were "a great many who have purchased for practical agricultural purposes, who are now satisfied they have given four times the value for their land." He was himself convinced that if the lands were now offered for sale, they would not bring as much as had been paid on their first installment. In Alabama many purchases seemed to have been made "under the influence of a sort of delirium," induced by many things—release of the Mississippi Stock, the activity of some seventy newly-established banks in Kentucky and Tennessee "whose paper was profusely scattered over the country," and the enticement of 25 cent cotton.

"It was the most discreet man sometimes who gave the highest prices," Walker continued. "I have known, for example, as high as seventy-eight dollars per acre given for land by those who bought it with the full intention themselves to cultivate it." If the system were changed to a cash basis, as was now proposed, great injury would be done to the many credit purchasers and to those planning to purchase land on credit. The government had a moral obligation, he insisted, to "interpose for the relief of the late purchasers." Many said it was time to stop, and he agreed, but he "would not violate the rights of those who had purchased under existing laws."[11]

New York's Senator King responded by approving conversion to a cash basis, but opposing Walker's amendment. He said he feared that every land purchaser would call on the government to review all his transactions and extend him relief. Furthermore, no one, he said, "would be found mad enough" to bid against a recent purchaser on the resale of surrendered land. Walker answered that if this were true, it would be equally true of land reverting under the current system. He felt his amendment would be favorable to the government, putting into the Treasury at once what otherwise would accrue over a ten-year period. He conceded that in Alabama "the former owners of land reverting or surrendered, would have a decided preference, and few would be found to bid against them." But he felt his plan to be the expedient one.

Sensing that the opinion of the Senate was against him, Walker temporarily withdrew his amendment. Six days later Senator Ninian Edwards of Illinois, with firm Western backing, introduced a pre-emption amendment which provided that a squatter be able to obtain a right to purchase any quarter-section "previously exposed to public sale . . . in the same manner and on such terms as were heretofore authorized by law." Edwards was of the opinion that the proposed modification of the system would be a boon to speculators. Believing that the sale of public lands should be confined to actual settlers, he wanted to continue the credit system on land previously offered for sale. His amendment was defeated, however, 31 to 12, with the Alabama Senators supporting it.[12]

Upon this defeat, Walker immediately moved that his amendment be considered and again took the floor, this time to describe the conditions in his state and elsewhere as an argument for his measure. In spite of his efforts, the Walker amendment was defeated by a vote of 29 to 8.

Walker and King of Alabama, Edwards and Jesse B. Thomas of Illinois, R. M. Johnson and William Logan of Kentucky, James Noble of Indiana, and William Smith of South Carolina supported the measure.[13]

Senator Edwards again moved the adoption of an amendment, this to provide that the squatter might purchase one quarter-section at private sale, "upon the same terms and conditions in every respect as have heretofore been provided by law." It was defeated, 28 to 8; significantly Walker and King voted against this amendment, which would have provided private sale for settlers before public auctions.[14]

Early in March, the land bill was given its second reading and passed by a vote of 31 to 7 to become the famous Land Law of 1820.[15] With its passage, the Sixteenth Congress closed its consideration of the land question. Walker was greatly disappointed. No substantial relief had been provided for those who needed it most, and a stream of letters from Alabama had testified convincingly to the importance of the problem at home. In January Israel Pickens, then register of the land office at St. Stephens, had written that a "debt of near 10 millions to be taken from our disposable means within 4 or 5 years will leave little behind." More than anything else, land relief would bring vigor and new life into the state. The solution he urged was authorization for settlers to abandon part of the original purchases of land and apply the initial payments to a smaller purchase.[16]

James Sanders Walker, engaged almost exclusively now in the buying and selling of land, wrote his brother in February from Coosawda, where he was visiting the dying Governor Bibb.[17] It was almost impossible at the time to make land sales even on credit to good men, he reported, especially those lands bought at the first sales and on which the second payments were due in August 1819, and the last, in August, 1821. He believed that this condition would continue until would-be purchasers saw some certainty of an extension of time for payments and a relinquishment of back interest. If Congress intended to act, the sooner the better, so "that we may know our fate," he wrote. "In the uncertainty, the lands belonging to the Government will not sell for more than one fourth of what they did two years ago—indeed there is not funds enough in the country to buy all that is offered even at two dollars an acre."[18]

Walker's amendment to the land bill had excited some enthusiasm at home, where, according to Thomas Percy, "the attention of all descriptions of people" was directed to the "obscure but to them important business of getting out of debt." But, he wrote in April, when it was rejected, that there was "no disappointment as it was thought that nothing so very desirable would pass."[19] Later in the year the *Alabama Republican* reviewed the problem in a lengthy article, noting that the lands in the big bend of the Tennessee River had sold for approximately $8,000,000. After the first payments were met successfully, cotton had dropped from 25 to 10 cents per pound, and "the common currency of the country [had become] so depreciated that $100 would only pay $85 debt at the land office. [Unless Congress takes some action] we hazard nothing in venturing the assertion that of the debt of 7 or 8 millions, which will be due at the expiration of five years from the purchase, not $100,000 will *ever* be paid." According to the *Republican* some of the best lands in the state had recently sold at $2.00 to $6.00 an acre on public sale, while adjoining lands two years before had brought $20 to $40 an acre. If Congress passed a measure authorizing the transfer of payments from one tract of land to another, the *Republican* predicted, one-fourth to one-third of the lands sold in the Madison County area "would be paid for at the enormous high prices at which they were bought," while the residue would revert to the federal government. But the editor "prayed" for a transfer measure, believing that it would enable the area to "become one of the most populous and productive in the United States."[20]

In January, 1821, Henry Hitchcock reported that Crawford's favorable views toward revision of the land laws would immeasurably increase his political strength in Alabama and the Western country.[21] The land issue was becoming one of paramount importance in practical politics.

One of Walker's first actions when Congress again convened was the introduction of a new relief bill which he thought would meet "the wants of all who have bought at any fair price and only want time," and would be "particularly calculated for the relief of Alabama—of those to whom more time would be unavailing." He wrote Tait that he felt it his "duty to relieve the state," if he could at the same time be consistent with the duty he owed the Union, for Alabama's position was unique. "We have given prices unheard of elsewhere," he said, "and our distress—being greater, the relief which would be effectual for the other new states would be far from being so for us."[22]

Walker's new measure, essentially the same as that he had offered in the previous session, included provisions for relinquishment, resale by the government, and return to the original holder of all proceeds received above $1.25 an acre up to the amount he had paid the government. One additional feature called for an extension of credit to those choosing to retain all or a part of their lands. A discount of three-eighths of the purchase price and interest was to be made for prompt payments, and lesser amounts as the time was extended.

Senator Johnson of Kentucky opened the discussion of the issue in the Senate's new session by presenting a resolution which provided that a purchaser might retain as much land as his payments covered at the original purchase price, with the remainder to be forfeited. But the great speculation years had been 1818 and 1819, and on these land purchases only one-fourth of the price had as yet been paid. Johnson's resolution would have resulted in these purchasers losing three-fourths of their lands.[23]

On December 28, the Committee on Public Lands reported a bill containing many of Walker's recommendations, among them relinquishment, extension of credit, remission of interest, and a discount *on the balance due.* Walker successfully opposed an effort of Tennessee's J. H. Eaton to restrict relief to natural settlers, and in turn was defeated in an effort to have the discount apply to the entire purchase price instead of to the amount due. He and King cast the deciding votes to prevent substituting 25 for 37½ per cent as the discount rate given for immediate, complete payment.[24]

In support of the new bill, Walker delivered the longest and most eloquent speech of his career. To thwart an undercurrent of objections in the Senate, he first voiced the arguments which threatened the bill with recommitment and attempted to refute them. Thus, to those who said the bill provided no aid for purchasers of land before 1817, he answered that since these earlier purchasers had already repeatedly received relief, their need was less.

Later purchasers were "better entitled to relief than others
because they [had] purchased at enormous prices." The
situation in Alabama was "peculiar . . . critical . . .
deplorable." Relief that would be effective in other states
would not be sufficient here. Time would do nothing for
her. But the question was larger than Alabama; it was "a
great national question" which concerned "the paramount
interests of the entire Confederacy." A system must be
framed, Walker said, which would encompass the national
problem, subordinating particular hardships to it.[25]

A number of Senators were concerned that the bill
confine all relief to actual settlers. From their point of
view, any land purchasers who had not settled on their
land were "speculators," and the desire to punish speculation was strong. Walker handled this objection with flattery. "I know this Senate too well; I have too high a respect
for its intelligence and liberality to suppose, for a moment,
that it is in danger of being misled by a *name*." He could
see nothing in the situation to warrant the Congress
making such a distinction. To give actual settlers such a
premium would be to provide a "bounty for removing
from the old States to the new." The argument seemed to
presuppose, he declared, that there was merit in such
removal. In regard to the new states, he went on, the
Congress had viewed the public lands as the domain of the
nation. "Your object has been to *sell* them for the highest
price," Walker insisted. All the world had been invited to
the auction, the only condition being that the highest
bidder would get the land. Congress, to further this policy,
had declared "that the lands of non-residents shall never be
taxed higher than the lands of residents," and on many
occasions it had refused "any particular advantages to
squatters." He wondered if the gentlemen would "make a

difference after the sale" which they had not made before it.

Some objected that the bill extended its benefits to town sites, holding that these had been pockets of speculation and should be beyond the pale of relief. But who has been the main profiteer from this speculation, Walker asked. "Your Treasury, sir. Yes, sir, the Government is, in reality, the great land speculator. Your system is built upon speculation." If speculation were a sin, the government was the chief sinner. It should first do penance before it sought to punish others.[26]

For politicians, the speech hinted that new power centers threatened. The credit system had developed a 22 million dollar debt, a debt which was concentrated in the new states, he warned the Senate. Tending naturally to be drawn together by common interests, these new states already claimed one-third of the representation in the lower house. What might be the result if the debt had been allowed to reach $100,000,000? Fortunately the credit system had been abolished, but what of the existing debt? One answer, he continued, lay in the privilege of transfer; it provided "an admirable expedient for lessening the debt, without sacrificing the interest of either party." More important to Alabama than all the other provisions of the bill, it would enable her people to save some of their land and get out of debt.

Allowing a deduction of three-eights for prompt payment would aid greatly, but, of course, the extent of aid would depend upon the time of payment. Of one thing he was convinced, Walker told the Senate. "More money will be obtained by the bill than ever would be obtained without it. Five-eights of the purchase-money is much more than Alabama's lands could be sold for."

Moving toward a climax, Walker listed some isolated facts indicative of the conditions which made relief imperative. Credit purchasers had calculated on the indefinite continuance of the credit system and were now caught short because Congress had abolished it, thereby causing land prices to plummet. By act of Congress the value of the article sold had diminished in the hands of the purchaser.[27] Furthermore, records showed the inequality in the prices of land. The nearly fifteen million acres sold outside of Alabama were bought for $28,741,886, while the 3,646,857 acres in Alabama had sold at $15,312,565. Again, unsound banks in Kentucky and Tennessee had flooded Alabama with paper, and Congress had added to this abundance by floating four million dollars worth of Mississippi Stock, receivable for lands only in Mississippi and Alabama. In these ways an artificial scarcity of land had been produced, and land prices had skyrocketed. Thereafter, the total currency of the Union had suddenly been reduced from $110,000,000 to $45,000,000—less than half. The seventy banks whose currency had flooded Alabama were closed; Mississippi Stock was nearly at par; and cotton prices had plunged from 25 to 10 cents per pound. Walker concluded in a great burst of eloquence and rhetoric:

> You have repudiated the seventy banks, and the planter who owes you must exchange one hundred dollars in these vile rags for eighty-five dollars of such as will pass at muster in the land office. I find it absurd to expect payment of $10,000,000 from a people living under such conditions. . . .
>
> The President recommends relief; your minister of Finance advises; your committee reports; the nation expects it. Individuals petition, nay whole States supplicate your clemency. . . . Seven of these new States and two

Territories await with solicitude the fate you are pre-
paring for them. . . . It is for you now to determine
whether they shall be stifled by the horrible incubus of
this debt, which presses upon their vitals, paralyzing their
energies, and arresting the wholesome play of their or-
gans; whether they shall be crushed by this gigantic
Colossus, which bestrides the vast and fertile region of
the West, with one foot in the Gulf of Mexico, and the
other I know not where—on the shores of the lakes, on
the summit of the Stoney Mountains, under whose "huge
legs" your fellow citizens in that quarter "must peep
about" to find the grave of their hopes and fortunes.[28]

Seldom has rhetoric been more effective. Shortly after
the conclusion of his speech, the land bill was enacted into
law. Walker had played a dominant part in securing
legislation said to be among the most important ever
passed by an American Congress.

It is interesting to speculate on the extent to which
Walker was motivated by the precarious position of his
brother. Not himself a land speculator, he had certainly
defended speculators, urging that they receive the full
benefits of the law. Three months earlier, James Sanders
had written from Montgomery that he had been unable to
sell a single acre of land during his trip south. Now he
reported that the passage of the relief law had made it
possible for him to dispose profitably of his highest priced
lands, including purchases in the "Big Bend" of the
Alabama River. He contemplated a trip to Pensacola and
Mobile where he would "make some speculations" if he
could find an opening. He assured his conservative brother
that his main attention was now directed "toward Coffee
and Negroes,"[29] but any such new direction proved ephemeral. By September he was deep in land speculation again,

and complained that his investment funds were reduced nearly one-half when the Tuscaloosa land office refused to accept notes of the Planters and Merchants Bank of Huntsville. He had been forced to leave without buying one particularly valuable settlement in the area, but resolved to return for it later in the fall.[30] By the end of November he had been able to acquire "some 50 to 60 town lots in Tuscaloosa!"[31] However inadvertently, Walker's land bill had certainly benefited his brother.

Personal motivation aside, Walker's contributions to land relief had made him a popular hero in Alabama. Charles Tait, judge and planter, was as happy as any speculator when he learned of the bill's passage. He pronounced Walker's speech "classical, eloquent and masterly." Everywhere in the southern portion of the state it had received "universal approbation and applause."

Tait found the law generally approved, and in his opinion it and the speech had "increased and fixed" permanently Walker's popularity. "Indeed it cannot be otherwise," he wrote. It must "give you a weight and standing in the Senate and about the government of which every Alabamian should be proud." He urged Walker to "go on in this way—persevere in the course you have begun and (if God should spare your life) you will leave a fame gratifying to your friends and which will be a valuable heritage to your family."[32]

The Montgomery *Republican,* upon the publication of Walker's address, held that its "masterful contents furnished a just estimate of the public worth of that gentleman."[33] There was commendation everywhere. When Walker returned to Huntsville in April, 1821, he was honored by a public dinner at the Huntsville Inn. The *Alabama Republican* reported that it had seldom witnessed "a more numerous and respectable assemblage of persons" gathered to "testify their approbation of the conduct of a public servant" and commented on the "elegant and sumptuous dinner." It quoted a toast to Walker: "Our Guest, the Hon. John W. Walker—May the gratitude of his constituents be commensurate with the important services he has rendered!"

Walker's reply throws some light on his views as to the nature and function of public service. In his opinion, he said, the fate of Alabama had rested on land relief. Absolutely essential to Alabama's prosperity, "it was not forbidden by a proper regard to the true interests of the Union." Much had been gained by the new act, and he hoped that the people would "entertain towards the general government the proper feeling of gratitude for its paternal care and kindness, and for the liberal course it pursued."

In liberality, the relief law had, he said, gone beyond what even its friends had anticipated when Congress first convened. "What liberated the fortunes of some, and gave fresh stimulus to the industry of more could not fail to increase [Alabama's] wealth and resources." Yet he warned his audience that only when they had extinguished the land debt and "not before" would Alabama "be the mistress of her vast resources." For himself, he had every reason to hold the "deepest solicitude" for Alabama's "advancement and prosperity." As her Senator he "had endeavored, with steadiness, with zeal, and with fidelity" to perform what he "held to be his duty." He concluded with a toast: "The State of Alabama!—May she always be more distinguished by the virtue, the intelligence, and the patriotism of her sons, than by the fertility of her soil, or the advantages of her position."[34]

Alabama and the nation had good reason to be grateful

to John Williams Walker. The Land Law of 1821, which he fathered, became a model for land relief legislation throughout the next decade. By September 30, 1821, which was the deadline for taking advantage of the Act, the land debt had been reduced by more than half—to $11,957,430. Still, inadequate transportation and communication had prevented many land purchasers from acting. To aid them, two extensions of the time limit were granted, the first in 1822, the second in 1823. By 1824, additional credit had been obtained on some 3,588,558 acres of land on which $6,740,358 was due the government. Anticipating that much of this land would have to be forfeited unless action were taken, Congress passed the Land Law of 1824, which applied only to those who had taken a certificate of credit under one of the previous acts. Embodying Walker's principles of relinquishment, this Act provided that such creditors might relinquish a portion of their lands and apply what they had paid on this to the tract they kept, provided the relinquishment, or the relinquishment and additional cash, covered all the payments due. For payments made before April 10, 1825, a discount of 37½ per cent was given. Under this law, the land debt was reduced by almost four million dollars by June 30, 1825, and Congress renewed its provisions, in 1826 and 1828.[35]

By 1830, what has been called a new land philosophy had begun to emerge. Where heretofore the government had looked upon the public lands as a source of revenue, it now began to regard their administration as a means to encourage settlement. A new goal appeared—that of granting homesteads to settlers.[36] Three additional land laws were enacted providing privileges of pre-emption, these coming in 1830, 1831, and 1832.[37]

From all these relief measures, Alabama derived more

benefit than any other state. "Of the four and a half million acres relinquished under these acts, three-fourths were given up" within her boundaries. Similarly, under the terms of the Acts of 1830 and 1831, more citizens of Alabama than of any other state pre-empted relinquished lands. Many Alabama planters had tried, under the eight years of credit extended them in 1821, to hold on to their best land—much of it purchased at exorbitant prices. But the task frequently proved to be impossible, and gradually the lands reverted. Under the Acts of 1830 and 1831, reverted lands could be pre-empted at not over $3.50 an acre, including former payments, or at $1.25 an acre if originally purchased at $14 or less. Thus "a considerable quantity of high priced land in Alabama passed into private hands at only normal figures."[38]

A combination of statesmanship and political expediency had resulted in the land relief measures which were enacted between 1821 and 1832. These measures made it possible for the nation to reduce the indebtedness incurred under the Act of 1800 without injury to the citizens of the West and at an insignificant loss to the government.[39] For his role in initiating this national policy, John Williams Walker deserves full credit.

ELEVEN

The Way of the Flesh

WHEN THE MARKET CRASHED IN 1819, JOHN WILLIAMS Walker's cotton crop was estimated at 30,000 pounds—in ordinary times enough to bring him substantial returns.[1] As the months passed, however, it became increasingly clear that these were no ordinary times. Thomas Percy, beloved friend, brother-in-law, and manager-in-residence of the Walker plantation, reported in late 1819 that Colonel LeRoy Pope was buying some cotton as low as 8½ cents. Percy found that the best price he could get locally for Walker's cotton was 10 cents, and rather than take this, he negotiated an advance of 6½ cents for Walker from Pope, so that he could ship the cotton to other markets and perhaps secure better returns.[2]

At Walker's instructions, Percy sold some Negroes and inaugurated an effort to collect what he could of the debts owed Walker. "I have consulted McKinley on your claim against the Estate of Col. Newman," he wrote, "and he thinks the best course will be to bring a suit in chancery against the heirs." He also made an arrangement to pay $450 on one of Walker's accounts with the Cypress Land Company.[3]

Walker was hard-pressed to meet his obligations, but there were others whose situation was desperate. Larkin

Newby, a year earlier considered a wealthy man, was ruined. A director of the Fayetteville, North Carolina, branch of the United States Bank as well as a prosperous merchant, he had signed notes to aid his friends. When economic conditions became chaotic, his business dwindled to nothing, his debtors defaulted, and his creditors demanded their loans. Newby's sense of honor was such that he felt constrained to dispose of all his personal property to satisfy his creditors. Concern for his family prodded him to write Walker, "If every thing should be taken from me, is it in your power to save my wife and little ones from beggary?"[4] Walker hastened to reassure him. "Your wife and little ones shall *not* starve, while I can help it," he wrote. That such a man as Newby, "so prudent, so industrious, and so interprizing [sic]" should be a victim of such distress moved Walker deeply.[5] He wrote at length of conditions in Alabama and of their causes. Alabama, too, had "learned to speak of thousands and tens of thousands. . . . Our lands rose beyond belief, and all other descriptions of property kept pace with it. Extravagance was the order of the day. The mania of speculation was epidemic." He had not been "quite so mad as most of" his neighbors. He had bought no high priced lands, but he "went into Bank—where a planter ought never to go:—and when I shall get out again, Heaven only knows!" Had cotton been worth twenty cents and had he been able to collect the debts that were owed him, he would have been able to free himself. But, he wrote, "I have endorsed and there again I am in danger."[6]

There were other dangers. Walker's improvident young brother-in-law, Willis Pope, again and again pulled the family close to destruction. "I had the honor to have my name brot. before Mr. Natory Mead as an endorser on

Willis note to Mr. Ware. One of Willis's careless tricks,"
Thomas Percy wrote on one occasion.[7] But a far more
ominous predicament lurked. Willis had plunged the
"successful labor of years of industry in a single venture of
cotton" by purchasing the interest of his partner and
becoming entirely responsible for the debts of their firm.
By late February, 1820, he had fallen in arrears more than
$30,000 to a Mr. Downing for advances on his cotton. "I
pity him, and I pity some others who will have to smart
pretty severely for writing their names," said Percy.[8]

Walker estimated that Willis could not lose less than
$60,000, and "the family, Col. Percy and myself gave a
bond to indemnify Hickman [the partner] against those
debts," he wrote. Yet in all fairness he had to admit that at
the time Willis made the negotiations there seemed to be
little risk. "Everyone felt that Willis would clear 50,000$
by the speculation, and would be worth at least 150,000$."[9]
James Sanders Walker heard at Coosawda that two or three
$7,000 notes of Willis and his father which had been given
to Hickman had been protested. James prayed that Walker
would not suffer in the affair. When he heard rumors that a
United States Treasury check on the Huntsville Bank had
been refused, he consoled himself with the thought that
everyone would go down together. He was relieved that he
would have "associates in misery."[10]

Willis' flier made Walker's situation look grave indeed.
"Should God vouchsafe to deliver me from this pinch," he
wrote, "I shall take especial care hereafter how I expose my
little barque to so tempestuous a sea." Never having
"dabbled in speculations" himself, he felt chagrined to find
himself involved, however innocently, in the speculations
of another. He was a mere planter, who held a "very pretty
tract of land, and some twenty laboring slaves—independ-

ent of a rather unwieldy household establishment." He noted among the complications to his affairs the fact that "my family has been constantly growing on my hands; and besides my own, that of my sister Coleman, which is numerous and wholly destitute, is dependent on me for support." He had been "enabled to live comfortably, keeping a pretty good table and contriving to make" his income cover his expenditures; yet, somehow, he had gotten into debt, and he realized that he "could not have chosen a worse time for it." To get out "with some little skinning and loss of hair," while losing "few of the substantial comforts of life" was his only wish. Never having had any hope of riches, he had, however, hoped to enjoy an ample—even abundant—share of good living with his family.[11]

It was fortunate that Downing, Willis' principal creditor, was willing to settle on the most generous terms, advancing him a "considerable sum to be employed in trying his luck at another shipment of cotton *without security*." Percy had a long talk with Willis, and extracted from the young man assurance that neither he nor Walker would ever suffer because of him. "He says that he has the means of securing us and that he will keep them," Percy reported.[12]

The fall and winter of 1820-1821 seemed to compound Walker's troubles. In December, the Tennessee River at Ditto's Landing rose to a height six feet greater than had ever been seen before. It would have been a fine time for "sending off cotton," but a wet fall had resulted in much of Walker's crop remaining in the fields even after the turn of the year. In January, an influenza epidemic struck the Negro families, making field work impossible for many weeks, while much soiled cotton still remained in the bolls.[13]

Although Walker's 1820 crop would exceed by fifteen bales the harvest of the previous year, cotton prices were no better in Huntsville, and reports indicated that the price abroad was going from bad to worse.[14] By January, 1822, however, his position was somewhat better. Mr. Sales, his overseer, had processed 62 bales of cotton (evidently 300 pound bales), while approximately 25,000 pounds remained in the fields. Percy was sanguine enough to refuse 12 cents a pound for Walker's cotton in Huntsville, choosing to obtain an advance of 13½ cents from the Huntsville Bank and to ship it to New Orleans.[15] The tide appeared to have turned, and, given a few years at this rate, Walker would have been able to amass a sizable fortune.

While absence from his family caused him constant grief, there was little actual anxiety for their welfare. Walker was fortunate in Thomas Percy, in whom Matty and the children had a beloved protector. Percy looked in regularly on his sister-in-law and her family, performed what services he could for them, and kept Walker informed of their well-being. Usually he could report that "with the exception of some wry faces" being made by the children, everything was well at Oakland.[16] Occasionally Matty might have a "cursed toothache" or be indisposed by influenza.[17] At times however Matty so disguised her true feelings that Percy would have been completely fooled had it not been for his perceptive wife, Maria.[18] The relationship between Walker and Percy was the more satisfying because Percy viewed his guardianship as a labor of love. It was no chore, but a delight, to take "Madam and the children" into town, frequently along with the Percy family. He was pleased with any opportunity to visit Oakland. Yet in addition to his other duties, he was forced to be a "Physician in ordinary to two ladies and somewhere about 140 negroes and agent and negociator both for the home and foreign departments to a Senator in Congress [Walker] and a Professor of the university of Transylvania [Dr. Samuel Brown]."[19]

At the same time, both John Williams Walker and Matilda were miserable over their separation. Aware of this unhappiness, Percy wrote cheerful reports as long as he could. "Your good dame has kept up her spirits thus far tolerably well," he told Walker in late December, 1820,[20] but when Matty became ill with influenza early in January, he attributed her illness to lowness of spirit.[21] A few weeks later he wrote, "One thing I shall here tell you is that I shall not give my consent to you going to Washington *again* without taking at least your better half with you. . . . [A] man who has *such* a wife so loved and so loving has no business to be away over the hills 6 months in the year more than once in a life time." Only as "deputy to Matilda" did he make this declaration, he pointed out.[22]

Though loneliness was his constant companion in Washington, Walker was able to secure most comfortable lodgings there through Judge Tait, who insisted upon making over to him all rights to his old room at Dawson's Boarding House together with all the books and personal articles he had left there.[23] Walker moved into Room No. 1, while Senator Nathaniel Macon of North Carolina occupied No. 2. Their mess was enlarged by the membership of "the celebrated John Randolph, of Roanoke." Here Walker found congeniality and came to know some degree of contentment away from home. He made the acquaintance of three women, two Mrs. Smiths and "the young and fascinating . . . Miss Spain," who, he said, contributed to the vivacity of the conversation. A Mrs. Simkins often entertained the group by singing and accompanying herself

on the piano, and occasionally Congressman Thomas Butler of Louisiana joined them, playing violin or flute, or
singing with equal facility. A Miss Terrel and Miss Elliot,
"both tall, young and handsome" sometimes became a part
of the boarding house's "after-tea-concerts."[24] But any such
Washington group changes rapidly, and in the fall of 1820,
Butler was gone, Mrs. Simkins "played the economist" and
stayed home, and Senator Johnson of Louisiana, whom
Walker described as a "very good . . . quiet easy fel-
low . . ." unfortunately "decamped to be with Butler and
Brown and their wives." Congressmen Joseph Kent of
Maryland, Ballard Smith and James Jones of Virginia and
Senator King of Alabama were replacements in whom
Walker took great pleasure.[25]

A year later, however, Walker decided to take Percy's
advice. Matty and their newly born son, William Memorable, accompanied him to Washington. Already in the
North was Mary Jane, the eldest of the Walker children,
who had been taken to Pennsylvania the previous summer
by the Percys and Dr. Samuel Brown. She was enrolled,
along with Susan Brown and Susan's cousin Mary Ellis
from Natchez, in the school of Mrs. Sigoigne at Frankford,
near Philadelphia, where she would remain for the next
three years. "I am now learning french and like it very
much and expect I shall improve enough to speak it to
father next winter," she wrote her mother upon her
enrollment.[26] Mary Jane was sufficiently affectionate and
sufficiently lonely to write her parents weekly at first,[27] but
her homesickness receded as the school diversions
increased. Mrs. Sogoigne provided parties, and there were
such events as the 1822 Washington's Birthday Ball at Miss
Brugiere's, where she "danced the whole evening."[28]
Friends of the family called on her whenever they were

THE WAY OF THE FLESH

near Frankford, and Dr. Brown provided exciting ex-
cursions—to Burlington and to the circus—which were
highlights in the girl's life.[29]

The Walkers left their four older sons with the Percys,
secure in the knowledge that they would receive the
tenderest care. But a little over a week after their departure, young Charles Henry Walker was dead, the Percys'
infinite solicitude notwithstanding. The distraught Percy
wrote a detailed account of the boy's illness and death, but
he did not mail it, fearing the effect the news might have
on Matty, who had been in poor health. Instead, the letter
was sent North in the care of Louisiana Senator James
Brown, Dr. Sam Brown's brother, with instructions that it
be given to the boy's parents at some later date when Mrs.
Walker had recovered. Percy's account is noteworthy for
what it reveals of frontier medicine. Little Charles, he
wrote, had become fretful and ill on Friday, apparently
suffering with a cold. Percy had administered an emetic,
but the child's temperature continued to rise through the
next day, and, the following morning, a Dr. Fearn, one of
two local physicians, was summoned. Charles' temperature
was high, he was coughing, and could breathe only with
difficulty. Dr. Fearn gave the child a dose of calomel and a
large dose of castor oil, and departed, telling Percy there
was no need for him to remain. He left a mixture of
"antimonial wine and Paregoric" to sustain the effect of
the calomel and allay the cough, and advised Percy to
administer an emetic if the child's breathing became more
labored.

As Sunday afternoon approached, Percy saw that his
patient was worse. He tried the emetic and then sent for
the second area physician, Dr. Erskine. Blisters were applied to Charles' chest, ankles, and to the back of his neck.

Erskine remained until Tuesday afternoon, but Charles grew steadily worse, and Percy sent again for Dr. Fearn and for Mrs. Pope, the child's grandmother. Fearn felt that Charles' head was affected and applied a blister to his crown. This and all efforts proved vain, and Charles died the following afternoon.[30] He had been ill six days.

It was two months before the Walkers heard of Charles' death. Matty was stricken, and Walker was so affected that he had to discontinue his normal activities for a time. "I . . . am a man, and a husband, and a father, and the arrow of affliction is . . . in my heart," he wrote. He grieved that he and Matilda had been so far away from Charles and "were denied the poor comfort of watching his decline and soothing his agony." If he "could pour out" his heart "like water, . . . tears of blood" would gush from it. Never had any event shown him so clearly how "poor and blind we are."[31]

Nevertheless, he forced himself to emerge from this melancholy brooding. He resumed his duties in the Senate and continued with a limited correspondence, but his own health, always precarious, seemed undermined by the tragedy. Washington was not unaware of his condition. Upon the death of Rhode Island Senator James Burrill, Jr., the *National Intelligencer* recalled, "Walker walked pale and emaciated across the hall to pass the bier. 'I know what you are thinking,' he said to some of the Senators, whose countenances betrayed their emotion, their eyes glancing mournfully from the living to the dead—*'You are thinking it will be my turn next.'* " On another occasion a Massachusetts Senator was answering with animation a speech which Walker had just concluded. At a crucial point, Walker was seized with a fit of coughing which almost strangled him. The Senator on the floor took his seat at once, declaring that "he was incapable of pursuing his argument under such circumstances as those under which he beheld the gentleman from Alabama." "From day to day," a contemporary journal reported, "it was almost a matter of surprize [sic] to find him still among the living."[32]

Yet he and Matty carried on. In May, 1822, Matilda visited Philadelphia where she was joined by Mary Jane. Additional exercise here improved her health. "I am sure I never walked half as much in my life," she wrote. But her nerves were not "nearly so irritable" as when she was in Washington, and she was blessed with uninterrupted sleep. New friends and visits to the museum provided needed diversions for her.[33] From Huntsville, Tom Percy urged Walker to take her "on a short trip to the cities farther north" if for no other reason than "the acquirement of knowledge."[34] But when she rejoined her husband in Washington, home appeared too inviting, and they started at once for Alabama where their children and friends awaited them.[35]

Back in Huntsville, Walker's health steadily declined. On November 21, 1822, he wrote Governor Pickens resigning his position in the Senate. "The state of my health has been so precarious, and so much worse than usual during the past summer," he explained, "as to render it for some time doubtful whether I should be able to attend the approaching session of Congress. . . . I recognize the paramount claim of the State upon my services." He had remained at his station as long as he "enjoyed sufficient strength to discharge its functions," he said. A trip to Washington now would be imprudent, and a winter residence there unsafe. In the meantime he felt the state should not suffer nor lose a portion of its representations because of his infirmities. Under the circumstances he felt compelled to resign. He expressed gratitude "for the unmerited distinctions" which had been conferred upon him and prayed that the General Assembly in selecting his successor would "fix on an individual, who to equal zeal and devotion for the interests of Alabama . . . [would unite] happier talents and more vigorous health."[36]

Walker's resignation came as no surprise to the Georgia Faction. They had been seriously concerned about the possibility for some months. Crawford had written Charles Tait in September that he was "fearful that Major Walker will resign his seat in the senate. I hope, however," he continued, "that he will regulate his conduct by the prospect before him relative to his successor. I have heard nothing from him since he left Washington."[37] Unfortunately, Walker's health did not permit him to indulge in practical politics. Now, however, it became clear that neither Crawford nor Tait had ever given up aspiring to another Senate seat for Tait. The appointment as Alabama District Judge did not compensate for its loss, and Tait had never particularly cared for the position. "I have been so long from courts and from thinking on legal subjects," he had written in 1820, "that I shall approach the Bench again with real reluctance."[38]

In the late spring of 1822, Crawford had informed Tait that William Rufus King had said he expected either Tait or Alabama's William Crawford would succeed him.[39] Secretary Crawford did not know whether King meant this would come with or without his consent. It was rumored, Crawford added, that King expected a mission to South America. In any case, Crawford told Tait, "I wish most sincerely that you may return to the senate." He felt sure that Tait's recent marriage (ironically, to the widow of his old political enemy, John Griffin of Georgia) would present no obstacles, since he could bring his wife to Washington with him.

Walker's resignation forced the selection of two Senators upon the Alabama Legislature which met in the late fall of 1822. In conveying Walker's letter to the Assembly, Governor Pickens added "with much concern and regret, that extreme ill health" was the cause of "denying to the State a longer continuance of his services."[40] But the Legislature was not so grateful to Walker as to let gratitude interfere in political strategy, and the Georgia Faction met decisive defeats in the selection of successors. To fill Walker's unexpired term, the "People's Party" of Israel Pickens elected William Kelly over John McKinley, the Faction's candidate and a neighbor of Walker's in Madison County. Senator King was re-elected over William Crawford, the South Alabama "Georgia" leader.[41]

Secretary of the Treasury William H. Crawford was disturbed by the election results and distressed that reports were circulating in Washington concerning his interference in Alabama. The election proceedings had produced "feelings of great acerbity toward me, in the bosom of Wm. R. King; and I presume his colleague had already cherished the same feeling toward me," he wrote Tait.[42] "Reports had reached me before Colonel King's arrival that I had written letters to Alabama to prevent his election, directing that you should be elected, and declaring that he should be provided with a land office." When Colonel King arrived in Washington, Crawford hastened to him to deny the rumors. King professed his satisfaction when the Secretary falsely swore that he "had never interfered in the elections of any state except in those of the state of which I am a citizen."[43] The victor could afford to be magnanimous, and King was.

While the politicians squabbled, the only man who could have saved the Georgia Faction lay dying. A remarkably cold, wet winter contributed nothing to aid his recovery. Some time in the early spring of 1823,[44] death came to John Williams Walker, one of the state's most gifted servants. He was forty years old.

Huntsville, on being informed of Walker's death, called a citizens' meeting to draft suitable testimonials to their distinguished leader. They adopted the following resolutions:

> *Resolved,* That this meeting deeply deplore, in common with their fellow-citizens, the loss our country in general, and our infant state in particular, has sustained in the death of the late Hon. JOHN WILLIAMS WALKER, whose unsullied virtue in private, and distinguished services in public life, have secured to him the affections and confidence of his countrymen.
>
> *Resolved,* That we sympathise with the remaining members of his family; that we consider their misfortune as our misfortune; that we mourn for his loss as for the loss of a brother.
>
> *Resolved,* That a Committee be appointed to regulate the order of the procession of the citizens attending the funeral of the deceased.
>
> *Resolved,* That the proceedings of this meeting be published in the newspapers printed in Huntsville.[45]

From state and nation came messages of praise and sympathy. The *Alabama Republican* valued most the statement of the *National Intelligencer,* "truly descriptive of the man, and of his character," and coming "from

abroad—from persons that could have but slight opportunities of forming an estimate of the virtues of the
deceased. . . . It required something greatly above the
mediocrity of Senators to make so lasting and so highly
favorable an impression," the *Republican* wrote,[46] and
quoted the following:

> To say, that, in that station [as Senator], he enjoyed
> the respect and esteem of all who became acquainted
> with him, would be a faint expression of the sentiments
> inspired by his integrity, his talents, his independent
> spirit, his candor, his suavity of demeanor. The critical
> state of his health surrounded him with a deeper interest,
> and shed an autumnal light over the prominent traits of
> his character. When first known in public life, he was
> already affected with the pulmonary complaint which
> terminated his mortal career. He knew that he was doomed
> to an early grave, but he bore the dispensation of
> Providence with a firmness and fortitude which would
> have induced the belief, if he had been less known, that
> he was not aware of the nature of the disease. . . .
> Notwithstanding his weakness, however, Mr. Walker
> was unremitting in his attention to his public duties,
> and perhaps no man was ever so short a time in the
> Councils of his country, who left behind him more
> friends or a more enviable fame.[47]

The Legislature of Alabama concurred in the general
high praise of the state's first Senator, and when, on
December 26, 1823, a new county was erected in northwest
Alabama, it was named in honor of him.[48]

Of Walker's intimate friends, Larkin Newby perhaps
most eloquently expressed the general grief and sense of
personal loss. Walker, he declared, possessing talents of the
first order, "rose to a level with the first men of our
country, at an age when most statesmen have scarce pass'd

the threshold of public life. . . . [His] rapid and brilliant course may be fitly comp'd to the Meteor." Like that phenomenon, the brevity of his life rendered his accomplishments all the more brilliant.[49]

John Williams Walker left a considerable estate, greatly taxed by debts. Because he died intestate, it was not until 1831 that the Madison County Court secured the final settlement, the grand total of his personal property coming to $30,798.62½.[50] Bonds, notes, and stock amounted to $5,704.83.[51] But in 1830, Thomas Percy, the administrator, and Mrs. Walker, the administratrix, had received the sum of $36,200.69½ and had expended some $37,311. In order to enable the books to be successfully balanced at this juncture, Percy remitted to the estate his allowance as administrator, $1,086.[52] The next year the court ordered the sale of the Walker real property, with the result that the high bidder, Richard Holding, agreed to pay the estate $9,600 in three equal, annual payments.[53]

It is all too apparent that Walker suffered physically and financially for his lavish expenditures of time and effort in the service of his state. He left his widow and six children, the last of whom, Richard Wilde, was an infant,[54] little worldly wealth. What he did bequeath them in full measure was a heritage of distinguished service, one which they would notably embellish by their own subsequent careers.[55]

Notes

CHAPTER 1

1. Walker Family Tree. See also Leslie Stephens and Sir Sidney Lee (eds.), *The Dictionary of National Biography*, XX, 511-513.
2. *Colonial and State Records of North Carolina*, XVII, 633.
3. Manly W. Wellman, *The County of Warren, North Carolina, 1586-1917*, p. 167. In 1764 Bute County was formed from the St. John's Parish area of what had been Bertie District. Franklin and Warren counties were formed from Old Bute in 1778.
4. Archibald Henderson, *North Carolina, the Old State and the New*, I, 324, 445-446, 571.
5. Walker Family Tree.
6. See George M. Brydon, *Virginia's Mother Church and the Political Conditions Under Which It Grew*, I-II, *passim*.
7. Amelia County Court Records, Colonial Papers, Amelia County Courthouse, as reproduced in Lewis P. Little, *Imprisoned Preachers and Religious Liberty in Virginia*, pp. 51, 146-147.
8. *Virginia Gazette*, Dec. 22, 1768.
9. Garnett Ryland, *The Baptists of Virginia, 1699-1926*, p. 47.
10. Herbert C. Bradshaw, *History of Prince Edward County*, p. 78.
11. Little, p. 360.
12. Ryland, p. 79.
13. Little, pp. 148-149.
14. *Ibid.*, p. 54; John P. Kennedy (ed.), *Journal of the House of Burgesses of Virginia, 1770-1772*, pp. 160-161, 185-186, 188. At the same time it agreed to a similar petition from Amelia County.
15. Chesterfield County Court Order X Book, No. 5, pp. 306, 320-322, as reproduced in "Prosecution of Baptist Ministers, Chesterfield County, Virginia, 1771-'73," *The Virginia Magazine of History and Biography*, XI, No. 4 (Apr., 1904), 415-417; Little, pp. 360-362; Ryland, p. 79; William W. Henry, *Patrick Henry, Life, Correspondence*

and Speeches, I, 117-119; Francis E. Lutz, *Chesterfield, An Old Virginia County,* pp. 98-99.

CHAPTER 2

1. David Benedict, *History of the Baptist Denomination,* II, 389.
2. R. B. Semple, *History of the Rise and Progress of the Baptists in Virginia,* p. 82.
3. Benedict, II, 389.
4. Semple, pp. 387-388.
5. Ryland, pp. 87-88.
6. *Loc. cit.;* Henry, I, 317.
7. *Virginia Gazette,* March 28, 1777, Sept. 21, 1775; Ryland, pp. 104-108, 47. The last statement is reproduced by Ryland from Morgan Edwards, "Materials Toward A History of the Baptists in the Province of Virginia," original MS in possession of Allester G. Furman, Greenville, S.C.
8. Little, p. 364; Semple, pp. 387-388.
9. Semple, p. 388, contends that Walker fell into immorality in 1774 and was restored to full communion after expressing contrition but was later excluded again. This may be based on information supplied by Silas Mercer and his family. Jesse Mercer, a grandson of Silas Mercer, writing in *A History of the Georgia Baptist Association,* pp. 24-25, contends that though Jeremiah Walker was an "Apostle for truth and religious liberty in Virginia," he "yielded to temptation" and "fell into disgrace." Walker, according to Mercer, was "overwhelmed with a sense of guilt . . . [and] left Virginia and sought a refuge among strangers, in a strange land; but shame and conviction followed him; and after a short time he returned to aggrived [sic] and offended brethren (1791), made an humble confession, and besought them to forgive and restore him to their fellowship. Thus re-instated he returned to Georgia, sought and obtained a union with the brethren here; and from his self-loathing and deep humility, his burning zeal and powerful talents, he acquired again, a considerable reputation among the churches. But now he adopted the Arminian scheme of doctrines and began to build up the things he had in his better days attempted to destroy." Mercer attributed this to "a defiled conscience" and to pride. William Cathcart seems to adopt this account in his biography of Jeremiah in the *Baptist Encyclopedia,* p. 1202. Several factors cast doubt on its validity, however. According to Mercer the date of Walker's espousal of Arminianism would be some time after his confession in 1791; yet David Tinsley revealed that he was converted to this doctrine by Walker while he was imprisoned with him in 1773. (See Mercer, p.

25; Little, p. 446.) Since Walker joined in almost a community migration in his movement to Georgia, it would not appear that he was seeking a refuge "among strangers." Moreover, Walker enjoyed the highest esteem in the community before 1791, when he supposedly made his peace with the church. Since he died in 1792, it would not appear that there would have been sufficient time for him to have returned from Virginia, re-earned the respect of the brethren and then to have lost it again before his death. Silas Mercer's contempt for Jeremiah's theology may well have influenced the impression that Jesse Mercer received of one of Virginia's leading clergymen.

10. Walker Family Tree.

11. George R. Gilmer, *Sketches of Some of the First Settlers of Upper Georgia*, pp. 7-8; Bradshaw, p. 128; Brydon, II, 468. Walker was affluent enough in 1777 to advertise for the return of "a deep coloured bay mare" and a heifer which had strayed or had been stolen from his pasture. "If they were not stolen, it is probable they made toward the *Long Bridge* on *Chickahominy*," he stated. He promised $10.00 to any person who would deliver the animals "at Mrs. *Camp's* ordinary near *Williamsburg*, to Mr. *John Goodall* in *James City* or to the subscriber in *Amelia*," $5.00 for the return of one of the animals and $20.00 for the conviction of the thief. See *Virginia Gazette*, Oct. 31, 1777. Some portions of this and the following chapter appeared in Hugh C. Bailey, "The Petersburg Youth of John Williams Walker," *The Georgia Historical Quarterly*, XLIII (June, 1959), 123-137, and are used by permission.

12. Gilmer, pp. 7-8.

13. George G. Smith, *The Story of Georgia and the Georgia People*, p. 133; Eliza A. Bowen, *The Story of Wilkes County, Georgia*, p. 2; Robert P. Brooks, *History of Georgia*, p. 141.

14. Gilmer, p. 8, *passim*; George G. Smith, *The Life and Letters of James Osgood Andrew*, p. 18; Bowen, pp. 37, 57; James E. Callaway, *The Early Settlement of Georgia*, pp. 71-72; George G. Smith, *Story of Georgia*, pp. 139-140; Walter G. Cooper, *The Story of Georgia*, II, 242; Works Progress Administration, *The Story of Washington-Wilkes*, p. 27.

15. Charles C. Jones, *The Dead Towns of Georgia*, pp. 234-238; George White, *Statistics of the State of Georgia*, p. 228.

16. Jones, pp. 235, 237; Lucian L. Knight, *Georgia's Landmarks, Memorials and Legends*, pp. 721-722.

17. James E. Saunders, *Early Settlers of Alabama*, p. 238.

18. *Early Records of Georgia, Wilkes County*, abstracted and compiled by Grace G. Davidson, II, 59.

19. *Records of Elbert County, Georgia,* ed. Grace G. Davidson (*Historical Collections of the Georgia Chapters, Daughters of the American Revolution,* Vol. III) , pp. 153, 168.

20. Mercer, pp. 20-21, 139.

21. Smith, *Story of Georgia,* p. 167.

22. *Records of Elbert County,* pp. 5-6.

CHAPTER 3

1. John Williams Walker to Larkin Newby, March 23, 1799, Aug. 20, 1799, Feb. 11, 1803, Newby Papers, Duke University Library, Durham, N.C.

2. *Id.* to *id.,* Feb. 4, 1803, *ibid.*

3. *Id.* to *id.,* Nov. 9, 1804, *ibid.*

4. *Id.* to *id.,* Nov. 10, 1803, *ibid.*

5. *Id.* to *id.,* Feb. 4, 1803, *ibid.*

6. *Id.* to *id.,* Feb. 25, 1803, *ibid.*

7. *Id.* to *id.,* May 20, July 26, 1803, *ibid.*

8. *Id.* to *id.,* Dec. 2, 1803, May 10, 25, June 29, 1804, *ibid.*

9. *Id.* to *id.,* Feb. 25, Apr. 23, June 23, 1803, *ibid.;* Jones, p. 236.

10. Walker to Newby, Apr. 23, 1803, Newby Papers.

11. *Id.* to *id.,* Dec. 2, 1803, *ibid.*

12. *Id.* to *id.,* Sept. 22, 1803, *ibid.*

13. *Id.* to *id.,* Apr. 1, 1804, *ibid.*

14. *Id.* to *id.,* March 13, Apr. 23, 1803, *ibid.*

15. *Id.* to *id.,* May 4, 1803, *ibid.*

16. *Id.* to *id.,* Jan. 6, 1804, *ibid.*

17. Bishop Charles B. Galloway, "Lorenzo Dow in Mississippi," *Publications of the Mississippi Historical Society,* IV, 233, 236, 241-243. Dow donated the grounds of the Old Methodist Church at Washington, Mississippi Territory, to Jefferson College.

18. Walker to Newby, Oct. 27, 1803, Newby Papers.

19. Ezra Squire Tipple (ed.) , *The Heart of Asbury's Journal,* pp. 568, 581.

20. Walker to Charles Tait, Dec. 8, 1819, Tait Papers, Alabama Department of Archives and History, Montgomery.

21. Walker to Newby, June 30, 1803, Newby Papers.

22. *Id.* to *id.,* Sept. 2, 1803, *ibid.*

23. *Id.* to *id.,* Sept. 22, 1803, *ibid.*

24. *Id.* to *id.,* Jan. 6, 1804, *ibid.*

25. *Id.* to *id.,* June 30, 1803, *ibid.*

26. *Id.* to *id.,* Aug. 20, 1799, *ibid.*

27. *Id.* to *id.,* Nov. 10, 1803, *ibid.*

28. *Id.* to *id.*, Aug. 20, 1799, Newby Papers.

29. *Id.* to *id.*, March 29, May 25, 1800, *ibid.*

30. *Id.* to *id.*, July 22, 1803, *ibid.*

31. *Id.* to *id.*, Aug. 12, 1803, *ibid.*

32. *Id.* to *id.*, Sept. 2, 1803, *ibid.*

33. John W. to James S. Walker, Dec. 20, 1806, John W. Walker Papers, City Library, Huntsville, Alabama.

34. *Id.* to *id.*, Jan. 25, Feb. 27, 1807, Dec. 20, 1806, *ibid.*

35. *Id.* to *id.*, July 13, 1806, John W. Walker Papers, Alabama Department of Archives and History, Montgomery.

36. Walker to Newby, Feb. 11, 1803, Newby Papers.

37. *Id.* to *id.*, June 3, 1803, *ibid.*

38. Relinquishment documents in Walker Papers, Montgomery.

39. Walker to Newby, June 3, 1803, Newby Papers.

40. Receipts in Walker Papers, Montgomery.

41. John N. Waddel, *Memorials of Academic Life*, pp. 1-44; Margaret L. Coit, "Moses Waddel: A Light in the Wilderness," *The Georgia Review*, V (Jan., 1951), 34-47; E. M. Coulter, "The Anti-Bellum Academy Movement in Georgia," *Georgia Historical Quarterly*, V (Dec., 1921), 11-42; E. M. Coulter, "Franklin College As a Name for the University of Georgia," *ibid.*, XXXIV (Sept., 1950), 189-194. Waddel moved his Academy in 1804 to Willington, another town in Abbeville District, S.C. He became president of "Franklin College," the popular name for the University of Georgia, in 1819 and served for ten years. A portion of the remainder of this chapter appeared in Hugh C. Bailey, "The Up-Country Academies of Moses Waddel," *The Proceedings of the South Carolina Historical Association* (1959), pp. 36-43 and is used by permission.

42. Augustus B. Longstreet, *Master William Mitten*, p. 72.

43. *Ibid.*, pp. 124-126.

44. Cited in William M. Meigs, *The Life of John Caldwell Calhoun*, I, 63.

45. David Ramsay, *History of South Carolina*, II, 294.

46. Walker to Newby, Oct. 6, 1803, Newby Papers.

47. *Id.* to *id.*, June 30, July 22, 1803, *ibid.*

48. *Id.* to *id.*, Oct. 27, 1803, *ibid.*

49. *Id.* to *id.*, Feb. 11, Nov. 10, 1803, *ibid.*

50. *Id.* to *id.*, Nov. 10, 1803, May 10, 25, 1804, *ibid.*

51. *Id.* to *id.*, Aug. 20, 1799, May 20, 1803, *ibid.*

52. *Id.* to *id.*, Oct. 6, 1803, *ibid.*

53. *Id.* to *id.*, Apr. [?], 1804, *ibid.*

54. *Id.* to *id.*, Feb. 10, March 9, 1805, *ibid.*

55. *Id.* to *id.*, Jan. 28, Apr. 23, Dec. 2, 1803, *ibid.*

CHAPTER 4

1. Walker to Newby, Apr. 21, 1805, Newby Papers; John W. to James S. Walker, Apr. 17, 1805, Walker Papers, Huntsville.

2. *Loc. cit.*

3. Walker to Newby, Apr. 21, 1805, Newby Papers.

4. *Id.* to *id.*, May 21, 1805, Walker Papers, Montgomery; John W. to James S. Walker, Apr. 29, 1805, Walker Papers, Huntsville.

5. Walker to Newby, May 21, 1805, Newby Papers.

6. Thomas Jefferson Wertenbaker, *Princeton, 1746-1896,* pp. 49, 118-132.

7. John W. to James S. Walker, Apr. 29, 1805, Walker Papers, Huntsville.

8. Wertenbaker, pp. 134-135.

9. John W. to James S. Walker, Oct. 6, 1805, Walker Papers, Huntsville.

10. *Id.* to *id.*, Nov. 23, 1805, *ibid.;* Walker to Newby, Sept. 29, 1805, Newby Papers.

11. *Id.* to *id.*, Nov. 6, 1805, *ibid.*

12. John W. to James S. Walker, Nov. 23, 1805, Walker Papers, Huntsville. Walker used the word "slaying" but expressed doubt that it would be found in the "English lexicographer." He found that it belonged to the New England states where it was frequently used. "With *toat,* and a few other words, such as the verbs *loan* and *advocate,*" he wrote, "perhaps it may find a place in Noah Webster's expected Dictionary."

13. *Id.* to *id.*, Apr. 22, 1806, *ibid.*

14. *Id.* to *id.*, July 13, 1806, *ibid.*

15. *Id.* to *id.*, Aug. 16, 1806, *ibid.*

16. *Id.* to *id.*, Dec. 20, 1805.

17. *Loc. cit.*

18. Walker to Newby, June 2, 1806, Newby Papers.

19. John W. to James S. Walker, Aug. 19, 1805, Walker Papers, Huntsville.

20. *Id.* to *id.*, Oct. 14, 1806, *ibid.*

21. *Id.* to *id.*, Jan. 25, 1806, *ibid.*

22. *Id.* to *id.*, Oct. 14, 1806, *ibid.;* Walker to Newby, Nov. 29, 1806, Newby Papers.

23. *Id.* to *id.*, Jan. 25, 1807, *ibid.;* John W. to James S. Walker, Feb. 8, 1807, Walker Papers, Huntsville. In late February, 1807, Dr. W. W. Bibb arrived to assume his duties as a representative from Georgia. He watched for an opportunity, as did his friend Walker

for him, to address the House, "merely to show that he can make a speech."

24. *Loc. cit.*

25. *Id.* to *id.,* March 11, 1807, *ibid.*

26. *Loc. cit.*

27. *Id.* to *id.,* March 21, 24, 1807, *ibid.*

28. *Id.* to *id.,* March 11, 1807, *ibid.*

29. Walker to Newby, July 28, 1807, Newby Papers; John W. to James S. Walker, Feb. 29, 1808, Walker Papers, Huntsville.

30. *Id.* to *id.,* March 12, 1808, *ibid.*

31. *Loc. cit.*

32. Walker to Newby, May 4, 1808, Newby Papers; John W. to James S. Walker, May [?], 1808, Walker Papers, Huntsville.

33. *Loc. cit.*

34. Walker to Newby, Feb. 1, 1809, Newby Papers.

35. Dunbar Rowland, *History of Mississippi, the Heart of the South,* I, 432-440; John K. Bettersworth, *Mississippi: A History,* p. 143. Adam Hodgson noted the same characteristics when he visited Natchez in 1820. He was surprised to find that for two days he had been eating with the Governor of Mississippi at a common table "where there was a promiscuous assembly of merchants, agents and clerks." In the neighborhood of the city, however, he found families living in the style of the higher English classes. They had "polished manners, and respectable literary requirements. . . . Their houses are spacious and handsome," he wrote, "and their grounds are laid out like a forest park." He spent several days visiting these families and particularly enjoyed hearing his favorite melodies on the harp and pianoforte. "I could have fancied myself on the banks of the Lune or Mersey," he declared. See Adam Hodgson, *Letters from North America Written During A Tour in the United States and Canada,* I, 169-185.

36. Bettersworth, pp. 125, 151.

37. Bayless E. Hardin, "Dr. Preston W. Brown, 1775-1826, His Family and Descendants," *Filson Club History Quarterly,* XVIX (Jan., 1945), 3-28; Bayless E. Hardin, "Dr. Samuel Brown, 1769-1830, His Family and Descendants," *Filson Club History Quarterly,* XXVI (January, 1952), 7.

38. *Ibid.,* p. 12.

39. *Ibid.,* pp. 7, 12.

40. John W. to James S. Walker, Oct. 23, 1808, Walker Papers, Huntsville.

41. *Id.* to *id.,* Nov. 15, 1808, *ibid.*

42. Walker to Newby, Feb. 1, 1809, Newby Papers. John W. to James S. Walker, Feb. 1, 1809, Walker Papers, Huntsville.

43. *Loc. cit.*

44. *Id.* to *id.*, Nov. 15, 1808 and Feb. 1, 1809, *ibid.*

45. Walker to Newby, Feb. 1, 1809, Newby Papers.

46. John W. to James S. Walker, Apr. 21, 1809, Walker Papers, Huntsville.

47. *Id.* to *id.*, June 14, 1809, *ibid.*

48. See Chapter V.

49. John W. to James S. Walker, July 22, 1809, Walker Papers, Huntsville.

50. Walker to Newby, Aug. 21, 1809, Newby Papers.

51. *Id.* to *id.*, Oct. 25, 1809, *ibid.*

CHAPTER 5

1. Walker to Dr. Samuel Brown, May 10, 1810, Walker Papers, Montgomery; Walker to Newby, Dec. 13, 25, 1811, Newby Papers.

2. Edward C. Betts, *Early History of Huntsville, Alabama,* p. 13; Thomas J. Taylor, "Early History of Madison County, and Incidentally of North Alabama," *Alabama Historical Quarterly,* I (Summer, 1930) , 156-159, 162.

3. "Alabama State Tract Book, Madison County, Embraces all land sales to November 1, 1854 and all locations to October 1, 1854," p. 32; Madison County Deed Records, Vol. E, p. 109; Vol. H, p. 522.

4. Frances C. Roberts, "Background and Formative Period in the Great Bend and Madison County," p. 139; A. B. Moore, *History of Alabama,* p. 68; "Autobiography of Gideon Lincecum," *Publications of the Mississippi Historical Society* (1904) , p. 465.

5. James S. to John W. Walker, Dec. 1, 1810, Walker Papers, Conley Collection, Frederick, Md.

6. Walker to Newby, Dec. [25?], 1811, Newby Papers.

7. *Loc. cit.*

8. James S. to John W. Walker, Dec. 1, 1810, May 31, Oct. 26, 1811, March 25, 1814, Walker Papers, Conley Collection. On Dec. 1, 1810, he dispatched by wagon 162 pounds of coffee, one barrel of brown sugar, one barrel of soap, five pounds of sugar (apparently white) and 432 pounds of "groceries." The carrier, John Wetsel, charged four cents a pound for his services. He served as agent for the payment of a $500 note for Walker in October, 1811. He collected $25 for him from W. W. Bibb in 1811 and in 1814 invested $120 for him in the Washington Monument Lottery. (In this curious chance-selling enterprise, the returns were split three ways. The win-

ners, the promoters, and a fund to build a monument to George Washington shared the proceeds.)

9. Taylor, I, 149-156; Betts, pp. 7-10.

10. Taylor, I, 151-152. Population increased between 1809 and 1816 to 14,200. Of this number, 4,200 were slaves. A pronounced inflation in land values, sometimes ten-fold, took place. The author has prepared tables of the land and slave holdings in Madison County in 1810 and 1815, basing them on the Madison County Unpublished Tax Returns, 1810-1815. Walker owned twenty slaves in 1810 and 26 in 1816. Col. LeRoy Pope held 68 and 97 in the respective years. See also "Population of Mississippi Territory," in *Niles' Weekly Register,* XI (Sept. 1816-March, 1817), 388, 642, and Betts, p. 31.

11. James S. to John W. Walker, Nov. 6, 1810, Walker Papers, Conley Collection.

12. Betts, pp. 23-27; Taylor, I, 164-168. Taylor quotes a description of Huntsville and Madison County written by Walker in 1817. Said Walker: "Huntsville is situated about ten miles from the Tennessee River, immediately round one of the finest springs in the world, issuing from a fine perpendicular cliff fifty feet high, in a sheet of water one hundred feet wide in a semi-circle forming instantly a fine bold creek, which it is now confidently believed can at a trivial expense be rendered navigable for batteaux to the Tennessee. Each square contains two acres divided into half acre lots, so that every lot is a corner lot. The public square contains about three and a half acres, lying immediately back of the spring cliff. On this are a court house, and market of brick and a small wooden jail. The first lot was sold on the 4th of July, so that the whole town is the growth of six years. In the suburbs are five cotton gins.

"The latitude of 35 degrees, which is the southern boundary of the State of Tennessee, bounds it [Madison County] on the north, on the other sides it is surrounded by the Cherokee and Chickasaw Tribes. The public land sales commenced in August, 1809. Its settlement and improvement have been rapid almost beyond parallel, and the price of land has advanced amazingly. The soil is for the most part excellent and admirably adaptable to the culture of cotton, corn, wheat and tobacco. Cotton is the staple, of which the average product is one thousand pounds per acre. Upwards of five thousand bales were shipped down the river last season besides a considerable quantity sent to Kentucky and elsewhere by wagons. The seat of justice is Huntsville. The face of the country is the most beautiful in the world, being in the main a level plain yet affording many mountain prospects and much romantic scenery. Its water courses are perma-

nent and afford many sites for important machinery. There are upwards of twenty already. The county possesses upward of twenty cotton gins besides those in Huntsville, and many more will be erected
in the fall. The climate is healthful and in a high degree pleasant.
Nowhere do you see more children with ruddy faces. There are even
now about thirty stores in Huntsville, and the crop of cotton for
the present year will not be less than eight thousand bales."

13. Walker to Dr. Samuel Brown, May 25, 1810, Walker Papers,
Montgomery.

14. Betts, pp. 14-21; Taylor, I, 167.

15. "Minute Book of the Superior Court of Law and Equity for
Madison County, Mississippi Territory, 1811-1816," pp. 21-24, 26, 28,
31, 37, 63. Though of major importance, the "Superior Court" was
not the first court convened in Madison County. In January, 1810,
LeRoy Pope convened the "Inferior Court" of five "Justices of the
Quorum," Madison's first court. It was organized under the laws of
the Mississippi Territory and was a replica of similar Virginia and
English institutions. See Taylor, I (Winter, 1930), 501. Betts, p. 21,
states that Walker "served as attorney-general at the first term of the
court" (Superior Court) of Madison County. This could refer to the
meeting in the fall of 1810 for which there are no records available;
Taylor, I (Winter, 1930), 498, states, however, that the fall meeting
was merely an organizational one in which provision was made for
selecting jurors for the spring session. He holds that Walker was Attorney General at the spring term, April, 1811, during which "many
civil cases appeared on the docket and criminal cases were taken
up on the third day." Furthermore, Taylor contends that Walker
served in the same capacity at a term of the court in 1812 (p. 500).
An examination of court records during the period, 1811-1816, however, indicates Walker's only service was that of a temporary nature
in October 1811.

16. "Minute Book," pp. 53-58; Taylor, I (Winter, 1930), 500, states
that a previous jury had failed to arrive at a decision in the case,
explaining the special session. He incorrectly places the date of the
latter as the second Monday in December; it convened on Tuesday,
Dec. 1.

17. Betts, pp. 18-21.

18. Walker to Newby, Dec. [25?], 1811, Newby Papers; Roberts,
pp. 304-305.

19. Ibid., pp. 234-236, citing Huntsville Weekly Mercury, July 7,
1915.

20. James S. to John W. Walker, May 31, 1811, Jan. 16, 1812,
Walker Papers, Conley Collection.

21. William A. Percy, *Lanterns on the Levee,* pp. 271-277. Three sons were born to the Percys. The third, William A., was the grandfather of the poet of the same name. Tom Percy purchased a Delta plantation for his sons, and they returned as grown men to Mississippi.

22. Brown remained in Huntsville until Susan, his daughter, was old enough in his opinion to be sent away to school. He then returned to Transylvania University to reorganize the medical school. In his six years at Transylvania Dr. Brown became one of the foremost medical pioneers in the United States. Hardin, "Sam Brown," pp. 8-10.

23. James S. to John W. Walker, Apr. 10, June 22, 1814, Walker Papers, Conley Collection.

24. *Id.* to *id.,* Aug. 5, Nov. 6, 1814, *ibid.*

25. *Id.* to *id.,* Nov. 8, 30, 1815, Dec. 12, 1815, March 19, Apr. 21, 1816, *ibid.*

26. *Id.* to *id.,* March 14, 1814, *ibid.;* Walker to Gen. John Coffee, Apr. 9, 1814, Walker Papers, Montgomery; four companies of Madison County militia participated in the campaign under Coffee and Jackson's command leading up to the events at Horseshoe Bend. See Taylor, I (Fall, 1930), 312-316.

27. Walker to Gen. John Coffee, July 16, 1814, Feb. 15, 1816, Walker Papers, Montgomery.

28. Andrew Jackson to President Monroe, June 11, 1817, in Clarence E. Carter (ed.), *The Territorial Papers of the United States,* XVIII, 111-112. The author has been unable to unearth record of a military position which would give Walker the title of major. It was probably a militia title and was scarcely more than honorary.

29. Petitions to Congress by Inhabitants of the Territory, Oct. 10, 1814, and Dec. 14, 1815, in Carter, VI, 449-461, 571.

30. J. F. H. Claiborne, *Mississippi, As A Province, Territory and State,* pp. 298-299, 350-351; Roberts, pp. 316-318. Even before Walker moved to the Mississippi Territory, Georgia's Representatives Howell Cobb, W. W. Bibb, D. Smelt, and George Troup (in March, 1810) recommended that should an additional judge be appointed in the Territory, Walker, "a young Gentleman of talents and respectability," be chosen U.S. Attorney in the new district. See Carter, VI, 51-52.

31. Tait to William H. Crawford, Apr. 22, 1813, Tait Papers. While in Paris Crawford wrote Tait (Oct. 12, 1814, *ibid.*) that he feared there was little patriotism left in America. "Party animosity in the eastern states has so deeply infected the minds of the Federal party in Massachusetts that they would much rather fight the Southern people than the enemy. So thoroughly am I disgusted with this class

of men that I would willingly consent that New England should separate if they would agree upon it among themselves."

32. Walker to Tait, Jan. 18, 1817, *ibid.*

33. *Id.* to *id.*, Sept. 21, 1817, *ibid.*

34. John Edgar Shipp, *Giant Days or the Life and Times of William H. Crawford*, p. 68; A. B. Moore, p. 99; Crawford to President-elect Monroe, March 3, 1817, in Carter, XVIII, 58-59.

35. *Loc. cit.*

36. Secretary Adams to Walker, Apr. 27, 1818, in Carter, XVIII, 33.

37. Walker to Tait, Sept. 21, 1817, Tait Papers.

38. Gov. Bibb to Secretary Adams, Feb. 16, 1818; Walker to Adams, May 23, 1818; Lund Washington to the Comptroller's Office, Oct. 7, 1819, in Carter, XVIII, 278, 334-335, 710, 711.

CHAPTER 6

1. *Journal of the House of Representatives of the Alabama Territory*, 1 As., 1 Sess., pp. 1 ff., hereinafter cited as *House Journal, Alabama Territory*.

2. *Ibid.*, pp. 21-23.

3. *Ibid.*, pp. 27, 35, 57, 114.

4. *Ibid.*, pp. 122-137; *Alabama Acts, First General Assembly, Alabama Territory*, 1 Sess., p. 105.

5. Ruth K. Nuermberger, "The 'Royal Party' in Early Alabama Politics," *The Alabama Review*, VI (Apr. and July, 1953), 81-98, 198-212; Roberts, pp. 329-330.

6. *Alabama Territory, House Journal*, 1 As., 1 Sess., pp. 100, 108.

7. *Ibid.*, pp. 92, 110; *Alabama Acts*, 1 Sess., p. 92; Walker to Tait, Sept. 22, 1818, Tait Papers. Though the territorial journals do not list the latter as approved, the memorial was forwarded to Senator Tait. Tait never received it, however, and Walker learned of its miscarriage too late to have the Legislature renew the petition.

8. *Alabama Territory, House Journal*, 1 As., 1 Sess., pp. 83, 94, 108, 120, 140; *Alabama Acts*, 1 Sess., pp. 89-90, 113, 24.

9. *Alabama Territory, House Journal*, 1 As., 2 Sess., pp. 44, 64; Walker to Tait, Nov. 9, 1818, Tait Papers.

10. *Id.* to *id.*, Sept. 22, Nov. 9, 1818, *ibid.*

11. *Loc. cit.*

12. W. W. Bibb to Tait, Sept. 19, 1818, *ibid.*; William H. Brantley, *Three Capitals, A Book about the First Three Capitals of Alabama*, p. 27.

13. Walker to Tait, Nov. 15, 1818, Tait Papers. The *Alabama Republican* (Dec. 5, 1818), was at a loss to find an explanation for the fixing of the seat of government "so far from the centre of popu-

lation and representation." The *Republican* found it contrary to the course of things under a republican government for a majority to be ruled by a minority. "We shall be prepared for any event however preposterous, when we see 28,000 yielding to the convenience of 21,000."

14. Bibb to Tait, Nov. 25, 1818, Tait Papers.

15. Walker to Tait, Nov. 15, 1818, *ibid.*

16. *Id.* to *id.,* Nov. 15, 20, 1818, *ibid.*

17. *Id.* to *id.,* Dec. 3, 1818, *ibid.* It was well Tait was in the Congress since the territorial delegate, John Crowell, seems to have opposed the plans of Walker and Tait. Walker wrote that he had no confidence in him. On one occasion Crowell remonstrated before a territorial committee against the rules for representation in the Alabama Constitutional Convention as adopted by the Alabama Territorial Legislature. See Walker to Tait, Feb. 8, 1819, and *Alabama Republican,* Feb. 6, 1819; also Thomas P. Abernethy, *The Formative Period in Alabama, 1815-1828,* p. 42.

18. Bibb to Tait, Jan. 8, 1819, Tait Papers.

19. Walker to Tait, Jan. 19, 1819, *ibid.*

20. *Id.* to *id.,* Feb. 8, 1819, *ibid.; Alabama Republican,* Apr. 17, 1819; Walker to W. W. Bibb, Sept. 28, 1819, W. W. Bibb Papers.

21. Secretary of State to Walker, March 26, June 14, 1819, and David Moore *et al.* to the Secretary of State, May 28, 1819, in Carter, XVIII, 592, 645, 636-637.

22. Walker to Tait, May 19, 1819, Tait Papers.

23. *Id.* to *id.,* June 17, 1819, *ibid.*

24. *Alabama Republican,* May 1, 1819.

25. *Ibid.,* June 5, 1819; Walker to Tait, June 17, 1819, Tait Papers.

26. "Notes Furnished A. J. Pickett by the Hon. John Dandridge Bibb in Relation to Governor W. W. Bibb and the Times in 1817-1818," Pickett Papers, hereinafter cited as "Bibb Notes," Pickett Papers, Alabama Department of Archives and History, Montgomery.

27. *Loc. cit.*

28. *Journal of the Convention of the Alabama Territory Begun July 5, 1819,* pp. 6-8, 12, 15, 19, 21, 24, 25-27, hereinafter cited as *Convention Journal.* Walker's personal correspondence was almost nonexistent during the Convention, and no official proceedings were published from the Committee of the Whole. Through July 22, the *Alabama Republican* reports the important developments in the latter.

29. No attempt is made here to summarize the provisions of the 1819 Constitution of the State of Alabama. Only those measures in

which Walker seemed to play a significant part are discussed. For a fuller discussion of the Convention and the Constitution which resulted, see Malcolm C. McMillan, "The Alabama Constitution of 1819; A Study of Constitution-Making on the Frontier," *The Alabama Review*, III (Oct. 1950) , 263-285, and *Convention Journal.*

30. McMillan, "Alabama Constitution," pp. 269-270, citing the Mobile *Commercial Register*, July 6, 8, 10, 1830.

31. *Constitution of the State of Alabama*, p. 7; *Convention Journal*, pp. 30, 32.

32. *Ibid.*, pp. 32-33.

33. *Ibid.*, pp. 22-23.

34. *Ibid.*, pp. 24-27.

35. *Ibid.*, p. 29.

36. *Alabama Republican*, July 15, 1819.

37. *Convention Journal*, p. 33; W. W. Bibb to Tait, July 14, 1819, Tait Papers.

38. *Convention Journal*, pp. 39-40.

39. Aug. 7, 1819, Tait Papers.

40. "Bibb Notes," Pickett Papers. This evaluation is in sharp contrast to that of the Convention's secretary, John Campbell. He wrote that Walker "knew little more of parliamentary proceedings than a 'friend's boy,' although he was an accomplished scholar and a man of some smartness." Campbell described Walker as "amazingly spoilt by flattery which is lavished upon him in our new country"; however, he privately conceded that the new Legislature would "send him to the senate of the United States" where he hoped that Walker "would equal the expectations of his friends." See John Campbell to Davis Campbell, Aug. 11, 1819 as cited in McMillan, "Alabama Constitution," p. 268.

41. Bibb to Tait, July 14, 1819, Tait Papers; Tait to Walker, Oct. 9, 1819, Walker Papers, Montgomery. I have dealt with this subject using some of this material in "John W. Walker and the 'Georgia Machine' in Early Alabama Politics," *The Alabama Review*, VIII (July, 1955) , 179-195.

42. Crawford to Tait, Nov. 7, 29, 1819, Tait Papers; Walker to Tait, Dec. 8, 20, 1819, May 14, 1820, *ibid.;* Tait to Walker, Oct. 9, Nov. 19, 1819, Walker Papers, Montgomery; Harry Toulmin to Walker, May 21, 1819, *ibid.;* A. B. Moore, p. 110; Abernethy, p. 113. Tait was confirmed by the Senate on May 13, 1820.

43. Bibb to Tait, Nov. 7, 1819, Tait Papers; Taylor, I (Winter, 1930) , 496.

44. A. B. Moore, pp. 111-112; John McKinley to Walker, Dec. 20, 1819, Walker Papers, Montgomery; J. W. Taylor to Walker, Dec. 8,

1819, *ibid.* McKinley arrived in time to run, unsuccessfully, for one of the circuit judgeships created by the Legislature. He did become a Trustee of the University of Alabama and, in 1837, an Associate Justice of the United States Supreme Court.

45. Bibb to Walker, Feb. 21, Apr. 13, 1820, *ibid.*

46. *Loc. cit.*

47. Tait to Bibb, March 26, 1820, W. W. Bibb Papers. Bibb replied to Tait (Apr. 15, 1820, Tait Papers) thanking him for this "very kind and affectionate letter."

48. Henry Hitchcock to Walker, Dec. 6, 1820 and Jan. 2, 1821, Walker Papers, Montgomery.

49. *Loc. cit.*

50. *Id.* to *id.,* Dec. 6, 1820, Jan. 5, 1821, *ibid.*

51. For a discussion of Pickens' career in Alabama, see Hugh C. Bailey, "Israel Pickens, People's Politician," *The Alabama Review,* XVII (Apr., 1964), 83-101.

52. Israel Pickens to Walker, Jan. 5, 1821, Walker Papers, Montgomery.

53. Hitchock to Walker, Jan. 2, 1821, *ibid.*

54. *Id.* to *id.,* Sept. 9, 1821, *ibid.*

CHAPTER 7

1. Newby to Walker, Dec. 24, 1819, Walker Papers, Montgomery.

2. Walker to Tait, Dec. 8, 1819, Tait Papers; Tait to Walker, Jan. 5, 1820, Walker Papers, Montgomery.

3. *Id.* to *id.,* Oct. 9, 1819, *ibid.*

4. *Annals of Congress,* 16th Cong., 1 Sess., 23, 35.

5. Walker to Tait, Dec. 8, 1819, Tait Papers, Montgomery; much of the remainder of this chapter appeared in Hugh C. Bailey, "Alabama Political Leaders and the Missouri Compromise," *The Alabama Review,* IX (Apr., 1956), 120-134, and is reprinted by permission.

6. Nathaniel Macon to Bolling Hall, Feb. 13, 1820, in Bolling Hall Papers, Alabama Department of Archives and History, Montgomery.

7. Walker to Tait, Dec. 8, 1819, Tait Papers.

8. *Loc. cit.*

9. Israel Pickens to Walker, Jan. 27, 1820, Walker Papers, Montgomery.

10. Tait to Walker, Jan. 5, 1820, Walker Papers, Montgomery.

11. *Loc. cit.*

12. Glover Moore, *The Missouri Controversy, 1819-1821,* pp. 56-57.

13. Calhoun to Tait, Oct. 26, 1820, Tait Papers.

14. Tait to Walker, Nov. 8, 1820, Walker Papers, Montgomery. The most recent historian of the Missouri dispute contends forcefully

that the "Northern solidarity of sentiment regarding slavery in Missouri only lasted from about November, 1819, to January, 1820." See Glover Moore, pp. 176 ff.

15. Tait to Walker, Jan. 5, 1820, Walker Papers, Montgomery.

16. Walker to Tait, Dec. 8, 1819, Tait Papers.

17. *Id.* to *id.,* Dec. 20, 1819, Tait Papers.

18. Henry Hitchcock to Walker, Jan. 2, 1821, Walker Papers, Montgomery.

19. Walker to Tait, Dec. 20, 1819, Tait Papers.

20. Percy to Walker, Jan. 25, 1820, Walker Papers, Montgomery.

21. *Id.* to *id.,* Nov. 17, 1819, *ibid.*

22. *Id.* to *id.,* Jan. 18, 1820, *ibid.*

23. *Id.* to *id.,* Feb. 8, 1820, *ibid.*

24. *Id.* to *id.,* Jan. 23, 1822, *ibid.*

25. *Id.* to *id.,* Sept. 4, 1821, *ibid.*

26. *Journal of the Senate of the United States,* 16th Cong., 1 Sess., pp. 102, 134, hereinafter cited as *Senate Journal.*

27. *Annals of Congress,* 16th Cong., 1 Sess., 424.

28. Glover Moore, pp. 107-110.

29. *Senate Journal,* 16th Cong., 1 Sess., pp. 164-166 and 189-190; Glover Moore, p. 89.

30. *Ibid.,* pp. 99-100.

31. Percy to Walker, Feb. 29, 1820, Walker Papers, Montgomery.

32. Walker to Tait, Feb. 11, 1820, Tait Papers.

33. Macon to Bolling Hall, Feb. 13, 1820, Bolling Hall Papers.

34. Walker to Tait, Feb. 11, 1820, Tait Papers.

35. *Loc. cit.*

36. Glover Moore, pp. 180-185.

37. Walker to Tait, Feb. 11, 1820, Tait Papers.

38. *Loc. cit.*

39. *Id.* to *id.,* Apr. 17, 1820, *ibid.*

40. Feb. 29, 1820, *ibid.*

41. Feb. 8, 1820, Walker Papers, Montgomery.

42. *Senate Journal,* 16th Cong., 1 Sess., pp. 200-202.

43. *Loc. cit.;* Glover Moore, pp. 100-103.

44. Apr. 17, 1820, Tait Papers.

45. Tait to Walker, March 23, 1820, Walker Papers, Montgomery.

46. *Id.* to *id.,* May 20, 1820, *ibid.*

47. Walker to Tait, Nov. 20, 1820, Tait Papers.

48. Tait to Walker, Nov. 8, 1820, Walker Papers, Montgomery.

49. Percy to Walker, Dec. 18, 1820, *ibid.*

50. Calhoun to Tait, Oct. 1, 1821, Tait Papers.

51. *Loc. cit.*

52. Writing to Charles Tait (June 3, 1822, in Tait Papers) in the heat of the political controversy prior to the election of 1824, William H. Crawford said that he felt that Southerners could play politics with the explosive Missouri question as well as the anti-slavery men. Crawford contended that John C. Calhoun had been "deeply impressed" with the idea that a geographical party had been formed which for several years would "control the course of events." Calhoun believed, according to Crawford, "that the election of an eastern President . . . would be more likely to secure the South the office of President in the year 1832 than if it had continued there until that period." Crawford felt that Calhoun was a realist who was attempting to exploit the situation as he found it.

53. Walker to Tait, Dec. 17, 1820, *ibid.*

54. To Tait, Jan. 28, 1821, *ibid.*

55. *Senate Journal,* 16th Cong., 2 Sess., 47.

56. Glover Moore, pp. 143-144, 219.

57. *Loc. cit.*

58. *Loc. cit.;* Clement Eaton, *A History of the Old South,* p. 215.

59. *Alabama Republican,* March 16, 1821.

CHAPTER 8

1. Carter, XVIII, 664-666; *Senate Journal,* 16th Cong., 2 Sess., pp. 211, 217, 226. This chapter originally appeared Hugh C. Bailey, "Alabama Political Leaders and the Acquisition of Florida," *The Florida Historical Quarterly,* XXXV (July, 1956), 17-29. It is used here in a re-written version by permission.

2. Samuel Bemis, *John Quincy Adams and the Foundations of American Foreign Policy,* pp. 300-316.

3. *Loc. cit.*

4. Calhoun to Tait, July 20, Sept. 5, 1818, Tait Papers.

5. July 20, 1818, *ibid.*

6. Sept. 5, 1818, *ibid.*

7. *Loc. cit.*

8. W. W. Bibb to Tait, Sept. 19, 1818, *ibid.*

9. Bemis, p. 315.

10. Crawford to Tait, Sept. 17, 1822, Tait Papers.

11. *Id.* to *id.,* Nov. 15, 1819, *ibid.*

12. Cobb to Tait, March 8, 1822, *ibid.*

13. See Chapter IX for Walker's evaluation of presidential hopefuls and their chances in 1822.

14. Bemis, pp. 317-340. The boundary line ran from the mouth of the Sabine River in an irregular northwestwardly fashion to the forty-second parallel, and thence due west to the Pacific Ocean.

15. Bemis, p. 350; Walker to Tait, Dec. 20, 1819, Tait Papers.
16. Crawford to Tait, Nov. 15, 1819, *ibid.*
17. Tait to Walker, Nov. 19, 1819, Walker Papers, Montgomery.
18. *Id.* to *id.*, Nov. 15, 1819, *ibid.*
19. Walker to Tait, Dec. 20, 1819, Walker Papers, Montgomery.
20. *Loc. cit.*
21. Bemis, p. 351.
22. *Loc. cit.*
23. Pickens to Walker, Jan. 27, 1820, Walker Papers, Montgomery.
24. Tait to Walker, Feb. 29, 1820, *ibid.*
25. *Loc. cit.*
26. Walker to Tait, Apr. 17, 1820, Tait Papers.
27. Bemis, pp. 351-352.
28. Walker to Tait, Apr. 17, 1820, Tait Papers.
29. *Id.* to *id.*, May 14, 1820, *ibid.*
30. Bemis, p. 352.
31. Calhoun to Tait, May 20, 1820, Tait Papers.
32. Walker to Tait, Dec. 17, 1820, *ibid.*
33. *Id.* to *id.*, Jan. 28, 1821, *ibid.*
34. *Loc. cit.;* Bemis, pp. 352-353.
35. Carter, XVIII, 664-666; *Senate Journal,* 16th Cong., 2 Sess., pp. 211, 217, 226.
36. Carter, XVIII, 664-666.
37. Tait to Walker, Nov. 16, 1821, Walker Papers, Montgomery.
38. *Senate Journal,* 16th Cong., 2 Sess., pp. 211, 217, 226.
39. Tait to Walker, Feb. 22, 1822, Walker Papers, Montgomery. Tait also requested that, if his judicial district were enlarged, an increase in pay be forthcoming, so that his stipend would be the same as that of the Mississippi judge.
40. J. H. Chaplin to Walker, July 13, 1822, Walker Papers, Montgomery.
41. *Senate Journal,* 17th Cong., 1 Sess., pp. 166-167. The boundary proposed for the territory to be annexed to Alabama was as follows: "Beginning at the mouth of the Perdido River; thence, up the same, to the thirty-first degree of north latitude; thence, along the said degree of latitude, to the middle of the Chattahouchie River; thence, along the middle of the said river Chattahouchie, or Apalachicola, to the Gulf of Mexico; thence, westwardly, including all adjacent islands dependent on the late province of West Florida, to the place of beginning. . . ."
42. *Loc. cit.*
43. Walker to Tait, March 19, 1822, Tait Papers.
44. *Loc. cit.*

CHAPTER 9

1. United States Constitution, Art. I, Sec. 8. A Bankruptcy Act was passed in 1800 and repealed in 1803; in 1841, and repealed eighteen months afterwards. Under the 1820 bill, never enacted, a principal creditor could initiate bankruptcy proceedings against a debtor (*Annals of Congress,* 16th Cong., 2 Sess., 272). The court appointed commissioners, who subsequently made an equal division of the debtor's assets and distributed them on an equal basis to all of his creditors (*ibid.,* 16th Cong., 1 Sess., 517). It was mandatory for two-thirds of the creditors to approve the division (*loc. cit.*). Commissioners were to have other powers, however, among them power to seize books and papers of bankrupts, and to detain their persons and to examine them as witnesses, so that they could be required to reveal all their obligations and assets (*ibid.,* 514). The bill authorized violent entry if the commissioners felt the bankrupt was attempting to conceal his true condition (*ibid.,* 520). When it was introduced, the bill made no provision for voluntary bankruptcy, but subsequently this provision was added in an amendment (*Niles' Weekly Register,* XVIII, 8). It seems clear that few provisions of the 1820 bill favored the debtor, but it did provide that a man could keep property he acquired after the conclusion of bankruptcy proceedings, and it also would have virtually eliminated imprisonment for debt, which was then not uncommon under makeshift state laws (*Annals,* 515). A debtor could also petition a United States circuit or district judge for a trial to prove he was not a bankrupt when a creditor had instituted proceedings against him (*ibid.,* 16th Cong., 2 Sess., 276).

2. See Chapter XI for an account of Walker's struggles to remain solvent.

3. Jan. 16, 1820, Newby Papers.

4. Newby to Walker, *loc. cit.* Notwithstanding Marshall, Newby contended that the Constitution had intended that Congress have the power to establish a national bank only in the District of Columbia.

5. *Id.* to *id.,* Feb. 27, 1820, *ibid.* Glover Moore, p. 332.

6. Walker to Newby, Feb. 13, 1820, Newby Papers.

7. Tait to Walker, Jan. 26, 1820, Walker Papers, Montgomery.

8. *Senate Journal,* 16th Cong., 1 Sess., pp. 242 and 272.

9. *Ibid.,* pp. 260-261.

10. *Ibid.,* p. 273.

11. *Ibid.,* p. 276; Glover Moore, p. 332.

12. *Senate Journal,* 16th Cong., 2 Sess., pp. 177, 185.

13. *Ibid.,* 16th Cong., 1 Sess., p. 185.

14. *Ibid.,* p. 194.

15. *Loc. cit.*

16. *Ibid.,* pp. 194, 203.

17. *Annals of Congress,* 16th Cong., 2 Sess., 1269-1270. It was not until 1898 that the first permanent federal law on the subject was passed.

18. We know that the last figure was a low estimate. See p. 151 and p. 162 *infra.*

19. Tait to Walker, Nov. 19, 1819, Walker Papers, Montgomery.

20. *Id.* to *id.,* Feb. 8, 1820, *ibid.*

21. *Id.* to *id.,* Feb. 29, and March 23, 1820, *ibid.*

22. Walker to Tait, Apr. 17, 1820, Tait Papers.

23. Mathew Carey (1760-1839), Irish-American publisher and political economist, who wrote many books and pamphlets favoring the national protective tariff and was the intellectual founder of the United States nationalist school of thought in economics (*New Century Cyclopedia of Names,* I, 816) .

24. Walker to Tait, Apr. 17, 1820, Tait Papers.

25. *Senate Journal,* 16th Cong., 1 Sess., pp. 315 and 318.

26. *Ibid.,* pp. 375-376. The Southern senators who opposed the bill were John H. Eaton of Tennessee, Outerbridge Horsey and Nicholas Van Dyke of Delaware, and Richard M. Johnson and William Logan of Kentucky. These same men had opposed postponing consideration of the army clothing bill. Defeat for the protectionists came through the formation of a coalition of Southern Democrats and New England Federalists. Ironically the latter, who probably represented the old mercantile class, had been among the most bitter in their condemnation of Northern Democrats for compromising with the South on the Missouri issue. See Glover Moore, pp. 319-331.

28. Henry Baldwin (1770-1844), representative from Connecticut and Chairman of the House Committee on Domestic Manufacturing, who was a strong advocate of a higher tariff (*DAB.,* I, 533-534) .

29. Gaillard to Walker, July 16, 1821, Walker Papers, Montgomery.

30. W. W. Bibb to Walker, Apr. 13, 1820, *ibid.*

31. James S. to John W. Walker, Dec. 6, 1820, *ibid.*

32. Memorial of the Legislature of Alabama, Dec. 17, 1821, *ibid.;* Israel Pickens to Walker, Dec. 20, 1821, *ibid.*

33. *Loc. cit.; Annals of Congress,* 17th Cong., 1 Sess., 142.

34. Walker to Tait, Jan. 19, 1819, Tait Papers.

35. *Loc. cit.*

36. *Senate Journal,* 16th Cong., 1 Sess., 337, 340, 369-370, 393.

37. *Ibid.,* 16th Cong., 2 Sess., p. 111; 17th Cong., 1 Sess., pp. 331, 348-349.

38. *Annals of Congress,* 16th Cong., 2 Sess., 154-155.

39. *Ibid.,* 16th Cong., 1 Sess., p. 26. At the time there were twelve Senate committees, their membership averaging five men each.

40. Walker to Tait, Apr. 17, 1820, Tait Papers.

41. *Id.* to *id.,* Jan. 28, 1821, *ibid.; Senate Journal,* 16th Cong., 2 Sess., pp. 275-277.

42. Walker to Tait, Jan. 28, 1821, Tait Papers.

43. *Loc. cit.*

44. *Id.* to *id.,* Jan. 19, 1819, *ibid.*

45. *Loc. cit.*

46. Crawford to Tait, September 17, 1822, *ibid.*

47. Walker to Tait, March 9, 1822, *ibid.*

48. *Loc. cit.* Nathaniel Macon wrote Tait (March 5, 1822, Tait Papers) that in his opinion the political principles which had brought Jefferson to the Presidency were forgotten. "The government was by him, managed for the good of the whole people, agriculture was not taxed to enable the rich to employ their capital in spinning and weaving or to enable the Speculation on bank credit to [es]tablish large factories, which could not be maintained." Macon thought that Crawford should be preferred by the Southern people to any other presidential candidate that had been named. "He will not be a Jefferson," Macon wrote. "I fear this bank vote will prevent it; to elect him will from present appearances require exertions, and his friends ought to be aware of it."

CHAPTER 10

1. *American State Papers,* III, 645. Much of the material in this chapter appeared in Hugh C. Bailey, "John W. Walker and the Land Laws of the 1820's," in *Agricultural History,* XXXII (Apr., 1958), 120-126, and is reprinted by permission.

2. Payson J. Treat, *The National Land System, 1785-1820,* pp. 102-103; Benjamin Hibbard, *A History of Our Public Land Policies,* p. 83.

3. Taylor, I (Winter, 1930), 489-495. The seven were Cotaco (now Morgan), Franklin, Limestone, Jackson, Lawrence, Lauderdale, and Blount.

4. Treat, p. 104.

5. According to Treat, the Mississippi Stock was issued to pay federal obligations to the State of Georgia and four land companies under the terms of the Yazoo Compromise, enacted in 1814. The background of this measure is given by Treat (pp. 356-366) of which the following is a greatly simplified and abbreviated version. In 1795, Georgia sold 35,000,000 acres of land, including the greater

part of the present states of Alabama and Mississippi, to four land companies: the Georgia, Georgia-Mississippi, Tennessee, and Upper Mississippi companies for $500,000. Coming at a time when six other states had ceded their claims to western lands to the Federal government, this sale roused ire everywhere, charges of corruption circulating within the state, and accusations being made outside it that Georgia had no clear title to the lands (p. 358). The Georgia legislature of 1796-1797 repealed the land sales. After prolonged dispute, Georgia ceded her right to the jurisdiction and soil of the lands in 1802, but in return demanded a payment from the government of $1,250,000 out of the first net proceeds of the land sales (p. 360). Once news of the settlement had circulated, claimants who had bought the land, including both private settlers and the four companies, turned to Congress for relief (p. 362), and finally, by Act of March 31, 1814, the government agreed to pay them $5,000,000 provided that they released all claims to the land. Individual claimants were allotted $250,000 of this sum, and the four land companies the remainder, with payments to be made in non-interest bearing stock payable out of the first moneys received for lands in the Mississippi Territory after the payment to Georgia was completed, but receivable in payment for public land sold within the territory in the proportion of $95 in scrip and $5.00 in cash for every $100 (p. 364). Such was the size of the land boom that the total amount due Georgia was paid by 1817, but it was 1820 before the United States Treasury began to redeem the Mississippi Stock in cash, paying then only 66 per cent of the value (p. 365), and by this time no land could be sold.

6. Tait to Walker, Oct. 16, 1820, Walker Papers, Montgomery.

7. *Loc. cit.*

8. For an account of Walker's own land purchases, see page 69, Chapter V.

9. *Senate Journal,* 16th Cong., 1 Sess., pp. 222-223.

10. *Annals of Congress,* 16th Cong., 1 Sess., 444-450; Treat, pp. 139-140.

11. *Annals of Congress,* 16th Cong., 1 Sess., 444-450.

12. *Ibid.,* 450, 458; *Senate Journal,* 16th Cong., 1 Sess., p. 190.

13. *Ibid.,* p. 217; *Annals of Congress,* 16th Cong., 1 Sess., 458, 481, 486, 489.

14. ". . . the revenue idea of administration was too strong to permit the sale of the choicest land at the minimum price to the lawbreaking pioneers [squatters]" (Treat, pp. 385-386). The six other Senators who had supported Walker's amendment, along with James

Brown and Henry Johnson of Louisiana, also supported Edward's amendment.

15. *Senate Journal,* 16th Cong., 1 Sess., pp. 222-223.

16. Israel Pickens to Walker, Jan. 5, 1820, Walker Papers, Montgomery.

17. James S. to John W. Walker, Feb. 22, 1820, *ibid.* Governor Bibb told James that he would have resigned if any man other than his brother Thomas had been President of the State Senate, and heir to his position. Thomas did succeed him shortly thereafter.

18. *Loc. cit.*

19. Thomas Percy to Walker, Apr. 5, 1820, Walker Papers, Montgomery.

20. *Alabama Republican,* Dec. 1, 1820.

21. Henry Hitchcock to Walker, Jan. 2, 1821, Walker Papers, Montgomery.

22. Walker to Tait, Nov. 20, 1820, Tait Papers.

23. Treat, p. 147.

24. *Ibid.,* pp. 148-149; *Senate Journal,* 16th Cong., 2 Sess., pp. 163-164.

25. *Annals of Congress,* 16th Cong., 2 Sess., 222.

26. *Ibid.,* 223-225.

27. *Ibid.,* 226-231.

28. *Ibid.,* 231-236.

29. James S. to John W. Walker, Jan. 28 and Apr. 21, 1821, Walker Papers, Montgomery.

30. *Id.* to *id.,* Sept. 25, 1821, *ibid.*

31. *Id.* to *id.,* Nov. 23, 1821, *ibid.*

32. Tait to Walker, Apr. 11, 1821, *ibid.*

33. Montgomery *Republican,* March 24, 1821.

34. *Alabama Republican,* Apr. 20, 1821.

35. Treat, pp. 152-160. In the spring of 1822, the Senate took up the House bill granting Missouri, Mississippi, and Alabama three per cent of the net proceeds of the sales of public lands in each state in accordance with the acts for their admission into the Union. An amendment to the House bill provided "the amount due to Georgia and the Yazoo claimants, under the Yazoo compromise (about five million dollars)," should be first deducted from this fund. Walker strongly opposed, contending this was a violation of the acts of admission. On April 3, 1822, the Senate disagreed with the House amendment. In Conference Committee the House members insisted on their amendment. On motion of Walker, the Senate resolved to insist on its disagreement. In a second conference, Walker, Williams

of Mississippi, and Eaton of Tennessee represented the Senate. The
House members still refused to give in, and the Conference Committee was forced to report the bill with a slightly modified amendment. On April 22, 1822, the Senate concurred. See *Annals*, 17th
Cong., 1 Sess., 353, 362, 393, 397, 427.

36. Treat, p. 386.

37. Treat, pp. 159-160.

38. Treat, pp. 158-159.

39. Roy M. Robbins, *Our Landed Heritage, The Public Domain,
1776-1936,* pp. 38-39.

CHAPTER 11

1. Percy to Walker, Jan. 18, 1820, Walker Papers, Montgomery.

2. *Id.* to *id., *Nov. 7, 1819, *ibid.; id.* to *id.,* Dec. 2, 1819, *ibid.*

3. *Id.* to *id.,* Jan. 18, Feb. 18, 1820, *ibid.*

4. Newby to Walker, Dec. 24, 1819, *ibid.*

5. Walker to Newby, Jan. 2, 1820, Newby Papers.

6. *Loc. cit.*

7. Percy to Walker, Jan. 25, 1820, Walker Papers, Montgomery.

8. *Id.* to *id.,* Feb. 29, 1820, *ibid.*

9. Walker to Newby, Jan. 2, 1820, Newby Papers.

10. James S. to John W. Walker, Feb. 22, 1820, Walker Papers,
Montgomery.

11. Walker to Newby, Jan. 2, 1820, Newby Papers.

12. Percy to Walker, Mar. 15, 1820, Walker Papers, Montgomery.

13. *Id.* to *id.,* Feb. 1, 1821, *ibid.*

14. James S. to John W. Walker, Nov. 20, 1820, *ibid.*

15. Percy to Walker, Jan. 15, 23, and Feb. 27, 1822, *ibid.*

16. *Id.* to *id.,* Nov. 17, 1819, *ibid.*

17. *Id.* to *id.,* Mar. 9, 1820 and Jan. 15, 1821, *ibid.*

18. *Id.* to *id.,* Jan. 15, 1821, *ibid.*

19. *Id.* to *id.,* Feb. 1, 1821, *ibid.*

20. *Id.* to *id.,* Dec. 30, 1820, *ibid.*

21. *Id.* to *id.,* Jan. 15, 1821, *ibid.*

22. *Id.* to *id.,* Mar. 9, 1820, *ibid.*

23. Tait to Walker, Oct. 9, 1819, *ibid.*

24. Walker to Tait, Feb. 11, 1820, Tait Papers.

25. *Id.* to *id.,* Dec. 20, 1820, *ibid.*

26. Mary J. Walker to Matilda Walker, July 30, 1821, Walker Papers, Montgomery. Mary Jane progressed well enough in her studies
to write numerous letters to her father in French and to read his
replies in the same language. (See Mary J. to John W. Walker,
Mar. 16, June 29, July 26, and Sept. 14, 1822, *ibid.*)

27. For an extended treatment of Mary Jane's experiences at school see Frank L. Owsley, "The Education of a Southern Frontier Girl," *The Alabama Review*, VI (Oct., 1953), 268-288; VII (Jan., 1954), 66-74.

28. Mary J. to John W. Walker, Feb. 22, 1822, Walker Papers, Montgomery.

29. Mary J. To Matilda Walker, July 20, 1822 and Sept. 25, 1822, *ibid.*

30. Percy to Walker, c/o Sen. James Brown, Nov. 7, 1821, *ibid.*

31. Walker to Tait, Jan. 27, 1822, Tait Papers.

32. *National Intelligencer,* as cited in the *Alabama Republican,* May 16, 1823.

33. Matilda to John W. Walker, May 5, 1822, Walker Papers, Montgomery.

34. Percy to Walker, Apr. 10, 1822, *ibid.*

35. *Id.* to *id.,* July 11, 1822, *ibid.* Percy made provision to ease the last few miles of the Walker's trip by the expedition of fresh horses to meet the weary pair.

36. Walker to Israel Pickens in *Journal of the Alabama House of Representatives,* 2 Leg., 2 Sess., pp. 47-48.

37. Crawford to Tait, Sept. 28, Tait Papers.

38. Tait to Thomas W. Cobb, Feb. 29, 1820, Walker Papers, Montgomery.

39. Crawford to Tait, June 3, 1822, Tait Papers.

40. *Journal of the Alabama House of Representatives,* 2 Leg., 2 Sess., pp. 47-48; Brantley, p. 113; A. B. Moore, p. 119.

41. *Journal of the Alabama House of Representatives,* 2 Leg., 2 Sess., pp. 80-83; Brantley, p. 113. In 1825, however, Kelly was defeated by Dr. Henry Chambers, who, in the interim, had become a supporter of Andrew Jackson. After 1819, the Georgia Faction was not able to elect a Governor, nor did they manage to elect any of the state's congressmen. Though the Faction remained something of a power within the Legislature after 1822, it was much weaker in popular elections. See Abernethy, pp. 103-106; Brantley, p. 113; A. B. Moore, p. 119.

42. Crawford to Tait, Feb. 16, 1823, Tait Papers.

43. For a view of some of Crawford's earlier activities in Alabama, see pp. 79-103 *supra.*

44. Montgomery *Republican,* Apr. 21, 1823, reports Walker died March 27; Thomas M. Owen, *History of Alabama,* IV, 1716, lists Apr. 23; the *Alabama Republican* of May 16, 1823, mourns his death.

45. Montgomery *Republican,* Apr. 28, 1823.

46. *Alabama Republican,* May 16, 1823.

47. *National Intelligencer,* as cited in the *Alabama Republican,* May 16, 1823.

48. *Acts of Alabama,* 5 Sess., pp. 82-84. Owen, II, 1373, and *Northern Alabama, Historical and Biographical,* pp. 171-172, incorrectly list the date of the admission of Walker County as December 20, 1824.

49. Newby to Matilda Walker, Apr. 29, 1823, Walker Papers, Montgomery.

50. "An Inventory and Appraisement of the Perishable Property of John W. Walker Deed, rendered on the 26th Day of May, 1823, pursuant to an order from the Honble County Court of Madison County, Alabama," in the Probate Court Records, Book 2 & 5, pp. 238-263. Included here were household furnishings. Those in the parlor amounted to $2,234.50, including a library of 950 volumes; the dining room's equipment was valued at $662.50 including four dozen wine glasses, a 52-piece "Tea-china" set with waiter, 104-piece set of ivory-handled knives and forks. In the children's room were 16 pairs of linen sheets, 24 flax linen towels, and so on. The gin house contained 52 saws valued at $100 and one old gin valued at $50. The meat house held 2,500 pounds of bacon valued at 10 cents a pound. The estate's 57 slaves varied extensively in price. Nine were valued at $600; five at $500; four at $450; one each at $675, $650, and $425; three each at $475 and $400; two at $525. One six-year-old boy was valued at $1,500, and a five-year-old at $1,100; the remainder were older people and infants whose prices were low; for example, 65-year-old Sally was valued at only $65.

51. Probate Court Records, Book 2 & 5, p. 517.

52. *Ibid.,* pp. 238-263.

53. *Ibid.,* p. 327.

54. Born in February, 1823, according to the Walker Family Tree.

55. Mary Jane married Dr. Richard Lee Fearn and became the mother of John Williams Walker Fearn who served the Confederacy as a diplomatic agent and as a colonel on General John Smith Preston's staff. After the war he served the United States government as Minister to Greece, Rumania, and Serbia, and then until his death as one of the judges of the Court of the First Instance, International Court, in Cairo, Egypt. He was survived by four children.

Percy Walker, the second of John Williams' children, was admitted to the bar after graduating from the University of Pennsylvania. After an initial career in the General Assembly of Alabama, he was elected to the U.S. House of Representatives in 1855. During the Civil War, he served the Confederacy as an adjutant and inspector-general with the rank of colonel. After the war he was appointed

Recorder of Mobile. All of his children were victims of tuberculosis and preceded him in death.

John James, the third child, was educated at the United States
Military Academy at West Point. After serving in the Creek and
Seminole conflicts of the 1830's, he became Collector of the Port
of Mobile for a number of years. During the entire Civil War, he
served as a colonel on the staff of General Braxton Bragg. After the
war, he was for a number of years Chief Justice of the Supreme Court
of Alabama, and later he was president of the Mobile and Ohio
Railroad. He died childless.

LeRoy Pope was born to John W. and Matilda on February 7, 1817.
He received his formal education at the hands of tutors and at the
University of Virginia and was admitted to the bar at an early age.
He attained distinction as a pleader and became a leader of his
profession in the state. After serving several terms as solicitor of his
circuit and as a member of the Assembly of Alabama, he returned to
private practice. In 1861 he served briefly as the Confederacy's first
Secretary of War; upon his resignation he accepted an appointment
as brigadier general in the Confederate Army. In 1864 he resigned
this commission and was appointed presiding judge of a military
court. After the war he returned to the private practice of law, and,
in 1875, was president of the state's fifth Convention, as his father had
been president of the first. Leroy was survived by three children, two
of whom died while young without issue; the third, Dr. Leroy Pope
Walker, Jr., practiced medicine in New York City for many years.
He died in 1940, leaving no heirs.

William Memorable Walker was born in 1821. He was educated
at Spring Hill College, Mobile, and the University of Virginia.
During the Mexican War he served as a first lieutenant of the "Third
Dragoons." In the Civil War he was a Captain, 1st Regiment Ar-
tillery, at Fort Morgan, Mobile Bay, where he died in 1864. He
never married.

Richard Wilde was educated at Spring Hill College, Mobile, the
University of Virginia, and graduated with honors from Princeton
University. He returned to Alabama to practice law in the early
1840's. Soon thereafter he was elected to the General Assembly and
was chosen Speaker of that House in 1855. In 1859 he was appointed
a Justice of the Supreme Court of Alabama, and later was elected
to a full term on the court. In 1861 he was elected a member-at-large
to the Provisional Congress of the Confederate States. In 1863, he was
elected to succeed C. C. Clay in the Confederate Senate, serving there
for the remainder of the war. He retired to the private practice of
law after the war and died in Huntsville in the 1870's. From his

surviving children most of the living descendants of John Williams Walker trace their ancestry. (Much of this information was derived from the Walker Family Tree; also see Owens, IV, 1717-1718.)

Of the Walker family, Edward Betts (page 86) wrote: "Few of the earliest families settling here, when Alabama was a territory, have been so continuously represented throughout these one hundred years by justly illustrious and worthy sons, as has this Walker family."

Bibliography

I. SOURCE MATERIALS

1. Official

A. FEDERAL

American State Papers. 38 vols. Washington: Gales and Seaton, 1832-1861.

Annals of the Congress of the United States, 1789-1825. Washington: Gales and Seaton, 1834-1856.

Carter, Clarence E. (ed.). *The Territorial Papers of the United States.* Washington: U.S. Government Printing Office, 1835-.

Congress of the United States, 69 Cong., 2 Sess. *Biographical Dictionary of the American Congress, 1774-1927.* Washington: U.S. Government Printing Office, 1927.

Journal of the Senate of the United States of America, 1819-1822. Washington: Gales and Seaton, 1819-1822.

B. STATE

Acts of Alabama, 5th Sess. Cahawba: William B. Allen & Company, 1824.

Alabama Acts, First General Assembly, Alabama Territory. Facsimile Reprint. Washington: T. L. Cole, 1912.

The Colonial and State Records of North Carolina. 30 vols. Goldsboro: Nash Brothers Printers, 1886-1914.

Journal of the Convention of the Alabama Territory Begun July 5, 1819. Huntsville: John Boardman, 1819.

Journal of the House of Representatives of the Alabama Territory. St. Stephens: Thomas Eastin, 1818. (The microfilm, Legislative Debates, Records of the States of the United States, ed. William S. Jenkins [Washington and Chapel Hill, 1949-], was used in reading this journal.)

Journals of the Alabama House of Representatives, 1819-1824.

Kennedy, John P. (ed.). *Journals of the House of Burgesses of Virginia, 1619-1776.* Richmond: Colonial Press, 1905-1915.

C. County

"Alabama State Tract Book, Madison County, Embraces all land sales to November 1, 1854, and all location to October 1, 1854." Supreme Court Library, Montgomery, Alabama.

Madison County Deed Records. Madison County Courthouse, Huntsville, Alabama.

Madison County Unpublished Tax Returns, 1810-1815. Mississippi Department of Archives and History, Jackson, Mississippi. Copies, Alabama Department of Archives and History, Montgomery, Alabama.

Madison County Will Records. Madison County Courthouse, Huntsville, Alabama.

"Minute Book of the Superior Court of Law and Equity for Madison County, Mississippi Territory, 1811-1816." Alabama Department of Archives and History, Montgomery, Alabama.

Probate Court Records. Madison County Courthouse, Huntsville, Alabama.

2. *Unofficial*

Bowen, Eliza. *The Story of Wilkes County, Georgia,* ed. Louise F. Hayes. Marietta: Continental Book Co., 1950.

Early Records of Georgia, Wilkes County, abstracted and compiled by Grace Gilliam Davidson. 2 vols. Macon: The J. W. Burke Co., 1932.

Gilmer, George R. *Sketches of Some of the First Settlers of Upper Georgia, of the Cherokees, and the Author.* Americus: American Book Co., 1926.

Historical Collections of the Georgia Chapters, Daughters of the American Revolution. 3 vols. Atlanta: Steins Printing Company, 1930.

Jameson, John Franklin (ed.) . *Correspondence of John C. Calhoun.* (American Historical Association *Report* for 1899, Vol. II.) Washington, 1900.

The Natchez Court Records, 1765-1805, Abstracts of Early Records. (The May Wilson McBee Collection, Vol. II) Ann Arbor: Edwards Brothers, Inc., 1953.

3. *Manuscripts*

A. J. Pickett Papers. Alabama Department of Archives and History, Montgomery, Alabama.

Bolling Hall Papers. Alabama Department of Archives and History,
Montgomery, Alabama.

Charles A. Tait Papers. Alabama Department of Archives and History, Montgomery, Alabama.

John Williams Walker Papers. Alabama Department of Archives and
History, Montgomery, Alabama.

John Williams Walker Papers. City Library, Huntsville, Alabama.

John Williams Walker Papers. In possession of Mrs. C. H. Conley, Jr.,
Frederick, Maryland, and her brothers and sisters. Typed copies
furnished the author.

Larkin Newby Papers. Flowers Collection. Duke University Library,
Durham, North Carolina.

Thomas W. and William W. Bibb Letter Books. Alabama Department
of Archives and History, Montgomery, Alabama.

Thomas W. Bibb Papers. Alabama Department of Archives and
History, Montgomery, Alabama.

Walker Family Tree. In possession of Mrs. C. H. Conley, Jr., Frederick, Maryland. Mrs. Conley, née Alice Patton Walker, is a great-
great-granddaughter of John Williams Walker.

William W. Bibb Papers. Alabama Department of Archives and
History, Montgomery, Alabama.

4. Newspapers and Periodicals
(Dates indicate files consulted)

Alabama Republican, 1818-1825.
Montgomery *Republican*, 1821-1826.
Niles' Weekly Register, 1811-1825.
Virginia Gazette, 1766-1780.

II. SECONDARY MATERIALS

1. Monographs

Abernethy, Thomas P. *The Formative Period in Alabama, 1815-1828.*
(History and Patriotic Series, No. 6 [Alabama State Department of
Archives and History].) Montgomery: Brown Printing Co., 1922.

Adams, Henry. *History of the United States During the Administra-
tions of Jefferson and Madison.* 9 vols. New York: Charles
Scribner's Sons, 1921.

Bagby, Rev. Alfred. *King and Queen County, Virginia.* New York and Washington: The Neale Publishing Co., 1908.

Bemis, Samuel Flagg. *John Quincy Adams and the Foundation of American Foreign Policy.* New York: Alfred A. Knopf, 1949.

Bell, Landon C. *The Old Free State, A Contribution to the History of Lunenburg County and Southside Virginia.* 2 vols. Richmond: William Byrd Press, 1927.

Bettersworth, John K. *Mississippi: A History.* Austin: The Steck Co., 1959.

Benedict, David. *A General History of the Baptist Denomination in America and Other Parts of the World.* New York: Lewis Colby and Co., 1848.

Betts, Edward C. *Early History of Huntsville, Alabama.* Montgomery: Brown Printing Co., 1916.

Bradshaw, Herbert Clarence. *History of Prince Edward County, Virginia—From its Earliest Settlement through its Establishment in 1754, To its Bicentennial Year.* Richmond: Dietz Press, 1955.

Brantley, William H. *Three Capitals, A Book About the First Three Capitals of Alabama, St. Stephens, Huntsville, & Cahawba, Including Information About the Politics, Laws, and Men of the Territory and State of Alabama, 1818 to 1826. Also Significant Historical Documents and Records.* Boston: The Merrymount Press, 1947.

Brewer, Willis. *Alabama: Her History, Resources, War Record, and Public Men. From 1540 to 1872.* Montgomery: Barrett and Brown, 1872.

Brooks, Robert Preston. *History of Georgia.* New York: Atkinson, Mentzer and Co., 1913.

Brydon, George Maclaren. *Virginia's Mother Church and the Political Conditions Under Which It Grew.* 2 vols. Richmond: Virginia Historical Society, 1947-.

Callaway, James E. *The Early Settlement of Georgia.* Athens: University of Georgia Press, 1949.

Campbell, Jesse H. *Georgia Baptists, Historical and Biographical.* Macon: J. W. Burke and Co., 1874.

Cathcart, William. *The Baptist Encyclopedia. A Dictionary of the Doctrines, Ordinances, Usages, Confessions of Faith, Sufferings, Labors, and Successes, and of the General History of the Baptist Denomination in All Lands. With Numerous Biographical Sketches of Distinguished American and Foreign Baptists, and A Supplement.* Philadelphia: L H. Everts, 1881.

Claiborne, J. F. H. *Mississippi, As A Province, Territory and State with Biographical Notices of Eminent Citizens.* Jackson: Power and Barksdale, 1880.

Cooper, Walter G. *The Story of Georgia.* 4 vols. New York: American Historical Association, 1938.

Coulter, E. Merton. *Georgia, A Short History.* Chapel Hill: University of North Carolina Press, 1947.

Eaton, Clement. *A History of the Old South.* New York: The Macmillan Co., 1950.

Harris, Malcolm H. *History of Louisa County, Virginia.* Richmond: Dietz Press, 1936.

Henderson, Archibald. *North Carolina, the Old State and the New.* 5 vols. Chicago: Lewis Publishing Co., 1941.

Henry, William Wirt. *Patrick Henry, Life, Correspondence and Speeches.* 3 vols. New York: Charles Scribner's Sons, 1891.

Hibbard, Benjamin H. *A History of the Public Land Policies.* New York: Peter Smith, 1939.

Hodgson, Adam. *Letters from North America Written During A Tour in the United States and Canada.* 2 vols. London: Hurst, Robinson and Co., 1824.

Jones, Charles G. *The Dead Towns of Georgia.* Savannah: Morning News Steam Printing House, 1878.

Knight, Lucian Lamar. *Georgia's Landmarks, Memorials and Legends.* Atlanta: Byrd Printing Co., 1914.

Little, Lewis Payton. *Imprisoned Preachers and Religious Liberty in Virginia—A Narrative Drawn Largely from the Official Records of Virginia Counties, Unpublished Manuscripts, Letters, and Other Original Sources.* Lynchburg: J. P. Bell, 1938.

Longstreet, Augustus B. *Master William Mitten: or A Youth of Brilliant Talents, Who Was Ruined by Bad Luck.* Macon, Ga.: Burke, Boykin and Co., 1864.

Lutz, Francis Earle. *Chesterfield, An Old Virginia County.* Richmond: William Byrd Press, 1954.

McMaster, John Bach. *A History of the People of the United States, from the Revolution to the Civil War.* 8 vols. New York: D. Appleton and Co., 1921.

McMillan, Malcolm Cook. *Constitutional Development in Alabama, 1798-1901: A Study in Politics, the Negro, and Sectionalism.* Chapel Hill: University of North Carolina Press, 1955.

Malone, Dumas, *et al.* (eds.) . *Dictionary of American Biography.* 22 vols. New York: Charles Scribner's Sons, 1928-1958.

Mercer, Jesse. *A History of the Georgia Baptist Association.* Washington, Ga., 1838.

Meigs, William M. *The Life of John Caldwell Calhoun.* 2 vols. New York: G. E. Stechert and Co., 1917.

Moore, Albert B. *History of Alabama.* University, Alabama: Alabama Book Store, 1934.

Moore, Glover. *The Missouri Controversy, 1819-1821.* Lexington: University of Kentucky Press, 1953.

Morse, Jedidiah. *The American Gazetteer, Exhibiting A Full Account of the Civil Divisions, Rivers, Harbours, Indian Tribes, &c. of the American Continent, Also of the West India and Other Appendant Islands; with a Particular Description of Louisana.* 2d ed. Charleston: Thomas and Andrews, 1804.

Mosteller, James Donovan. *A History of the Kiokee Baptist Church in Georgia.* Ann Arbor: Edwards Bros. Inc., 1952.

Northern Alabama, Historical and Biographical. Birmingham: Smith and Deland, 1888.

Owen, Thomas M. *History of Alabama and Dictionary of Alabama Biography.* 4 vols. Chicago: S. J. Clarke, 1921.

Owsley, Frank L. *Plain Folk of the Old South.* Baton Rouge: Louisiana State University Press, 1949.

Percy, William Alexander. *Lanterns on the Levee, Recollections of a Planter's Son.* New York: Alfred A. Knopf, 1941.

Pickett, James A. *History of Alabama and Incidentally of Georgia and Mississippi . . . from the Earliest Period.* 2 vols. Charleston: Walker and James, 1851.

Ramsay, David. *The History of South Carolina.* 2 vols. Charleston: David Longworth, 1809.

Robbins, Roy M. *Our Landed Heritage, The Public Domain, 1776-1936.* Princeton: Princeton University Press, 1942.

Roberts, Frances Cabaniss. "Background and Formative Period in the Great Bend and Madison County." Unpublished Ph.D. Dissertation, University of Alabama, 1956.

Rowland, Dunbar. *History of Mississippi, the Heart of the South.* 4 vols. Chicago and Jackson: S. J. Clarke, 1925.

Royall, Anne. *Letters from Alabama on Various Subjects to Which is Added An Appendix containing Remarks on Sundry Members of the 20th and 21st Congress and Other High Characters, &c. &c. at the Seat of Government.* Washington, 1830.

Ryland, Garnett. *The Baptists of Virginia, 1699-1926.* Richmond: The Virginia Baptist Board of Missions and Education, 1955.

Saunders, James E. *Early Settlers of Alabama.* New Orleans: L. Graham and Sons, 1899.

Sellers, James B. *History of the University of Alabama, 1818-1902.* Vol. I. University: University of Alabama Press, 1953.

Semple, Robert B. *History of the Rise and Progress of the Baptist in Virginia*. Richmond: John O'Lynch, 1810.

Shipp, John Edgar. *Giant Days or the Life and Times of William H. Crawford, Embracing also Excerpts from His Diary, Letters and Speeches together with a Copious Index to the Whole*. Americus, Ga.: Southern Printers, 1909.

Smith, George G. *The Life and Letters of James Osgood Andrew, Bishop of the Methodist Episcopal Church, South, with Glances at his Contemporaries and at Events in Church History*. Nashville: Southern Methodist Publishing House, 1882.

Smith. *The Story of Georgia and the Georgia People, 1732 to 1860*. Atlanta: Franklin Printing and Publishing Co., 1900.

Stephens, Leslie, and Lee, Sir Sidney (eds.). *The Dictionary of National Biography*. 20 vols. London: Oxford University Press, 1921.

Tipple, Ezra Squire (ed.). *The Heart of Asbury's Journal*. New York and Cincinnati: The Methodist Book Concern, 1904.

Townsend, Leah. *South Carolina Baptists, 1670-1805*. Florence: Florence Printing Co., 1935.

Treat, Payson J. *The National Land System, 1785-1820*. New York: E. B. Treat and Co., 1910.

Waddel, John N. *Memorials of Academic Life, Being an Historical Sketch of the Waddel Family, Identified through Three Generations with the History of the Higher Education in the South and Southwest*. Richmond: Presbyterian Committee of Publication, 1891.

Wade, John Donald. *Augustus Baldwin Longstreet, A Study of the Development of Culture in the South*. New York: The Macmillan Co., 1924.

Warden, David B. *A Statistical, Political and Historical Account of the United States of North America; from the Period of their First Colonization to the Present Day*. 3 vols. Edinburgh: Archibald Constable and Co., 1819.

Wellman, Manly Wade. *The County of Warren, North Carolina, 1586-1917*. Chapel Hill: University of North Carolina Press, 1959.

Wertenbaker, Thomas Jefferson. *Princeton, 1746-1896*. Princeton: Princeton University Press, 1946.

White, George. *Statistics of the State of Georgia: Including an Account of its Natural, Civil and Ecclesiastical History; Together with a particular Description of Each County, Notices of the Manners and Customs of its Aboriginal Tribes, and a Correct Map of the State*. Savannah: W. Thorne Williams, 1849.

Wiltse, Charles M. *John C. Calhoun, Nationalist, 1782-1828*. New York: The Bobbs-Merrill Co., 1944.

Wood, Marie Stevens Walker. *The Walker Heritage*. Macon, privately printed, 1956.

Works Progress Administration. *The Story of Washington-Wilkes.* Athens: University of Georgia Press, 1949.

———. *Dinwiddie County*. Dinwiddie County Schoolboard, 1942.

2. *Periodical Literature*

"Autobiography of Gideon Lincecum," *Publications of the Mississippi Historical Society* (1904), pp. 443-520.

Bailey, Hugh C. "Alabama Political Leaders and the Acquisition of Florida," *The Florida Historical Quarterly,* XXXV (July, 1956), 17-29.

———. "Alabama Political Leaders and the Missouri Compromise," *The Alabama Review,* IX (Apr., 1956), 120-134.

———. "Israel Pickens, People's Politician," *The Alabama Review,* XVII (Apr., 1964), 83-101.

———. "John W. Walker and the 'Georgia Machine' in Early Alabama Politics," *The Alabama Review,* VIII (July, 1955), 179-195.

———. "John W. Walker and the Land Laws of the 1820's," *Agricultural History,* XXXII (Apr., 1958), 120-126.

———. "The Petersburg Youth of John Williams Walker," *Georgia Historical Quarterly,* XLIII (June, 1959), 123-137.

———. "The Up-Country Academies of Moses Waddel," *The Proceedings of the South Carolina Historical Association* (1959), pp. 36-43.

Coit, Margaret L. "Moses Waddel: A Light in the Wilderness," *The Georgia Review,* V (Jan., 1951), 34-47.

Coulter, E. Merton. "The Ante-Bellum Academy Movement in Georgia," *Georgia Historical Quarterly,* V (Dec., 1921), 11-42.

———. "A Famous Duel that Was Never Fought," *Georgia Historical Quarterly,* XLIII (Dec., 1959), 365-377.

———. "Franklin College As a Name for the University of Georgia," *Georgia Historical Quarterly,* XXXIV (Sept., 1950), 187-194.

Galloway, Bishop Charles B. "Lorenzo Dow in Mississippi," *Publications of the Mississippi Historical Society,* ed. Franklin L. Riley, IV (1901), 233-244.

Hardin, Bayless E. "Dr. Preston W. Brown, 1775-1826, His Family and

Descendants," *Filson Club History Quarterly,* XVIX (Jan., 1954), 3-28.

———. "Dr. Samuel Brown, 1769-1830, His Family and Descendants," *Filson Club History Quarterly,* XXVI (Jan., 1952), 3-27.

Lyon, Ralph M. "Moses Waddel and the Willington Academy," *The North Carolina Historical Review,* VIII (Jan.–Oct., 1931), 284-300.

McMillan, Malcolm C. "The Alabama Constitution of 1819: A Study of Constitution-Making on the Frontier," *The Alabama Review,* III (Oct., 1950), 263-286.

Nuermberger, Ruth Ketring. "The 'Royal Party' in Early Alabama Politics," *The Alabama Review,* VI (Apr. and July, 1953), 81-98 and 198-212.

Owsley, Frank L. "The Education of a Southern Frontier Girl," *The Alabama Review,* VI (Oct., 1953), 268-288; VII (Jan., 1954), 66-74.

"Prosecution of Baptist Ministers, Chesterfield County, Virginia, 1771-'73," *The Virginia Magazine of History and Biography,* XI, No. 4 (Apr., 1904), 415-417.

Taylor, Thomas Jones. "Early History of Madison County, Alabama," *Alabama Historical Quarterly,* I (Spring–Winter, 1930), 101-111, 149-168, 308-317, 489-505; II (Spring, 1940), 86-91.

Index

DATE DUE

GAYLORD			PRINTED IN U.S.A.